AF560611

Reforming Secondary Education

Reforming Secondary Education

Editor

Dr. Digumarti Bhaskara Rao

M.Sc., M.A., M.A., M.Ed., Ph.D.

Reader

R.V.R. College of Education

Srinivasa Nagar Colony

Guntur–522 006

Andhra Pradesh (India)

DISCOVERY PUBLISHING HOUSE

NEW DELHI

First Published - 2004

Reprinted - 2014

ISBN: 978-81-7141-843-5

Reforming Secondary Education

Published by:

DISCOVERY PUBLISHING HOUSE PVT. LTD.

4383/4B, Ansari Road, Darya Ganj

New Delhi-110 002 (India)

Phone: +91-11-23279245, 43596064-65

Fax: +91-11-23253475

E-mail: discoverypublishinghouse@gmail.com

sales@discoverypublishinggroup.com

web: www.discoverypublishinggroup.com

Printed at:

Infinity Imaging Systems

Delhi

Dedicated
to my
beloved sister

Mrs. Vijaya Lakshmi
by
Dr. Bhaskara Rao

Preface

Secondary education is very much crucial as it is the connecting link between primary education and higher education. Recognising the very role and importance of secondary education, it is in its reform in various countries across the world. To give impetus to its transformation, the UNESCO is organising several regional meetings and international and conferences for identifying ways and means of reforming secondary education. This book is the result of such meetings and conferences in which the final outcomes formed part of it.

This book on reforming secondary education mainly presents the results of the International Conference on the Reform of Secondary Education and the Meeting of the Interagency Consultative Group on Secondary Education Reform and Youth Affairs that are becoming instrumental in the reform of secondary education.

I am thankful to the Ministry of Education, Sultanate of Oman; the UNESCO; Prof. Bill Mulford; and Prof. Jean Michel Leclercq for utilising their material and contributions in preparing this book.

Dr. Digumarti Bhaskara Rao
Sai Soudha
D-43, S.V.N. Colony
Guntur 522006
Andhra Pradesh
India

Contents

PART—2

SECONDARY EDUCATION REFORM AND YOUTH AFFAIRS

PART—3

GENERAL SECONDARY SCHOOL EDUCATION IN THE 21ST CENTURY

PART—3

Part-1

REFORM OF SECONDARY EDUCATION

International Conference on the Reform of Secondary Education—Secondary Education for a Better Future: Trends, Challenges and Priorities, 22-24 December 2002, Ministry of Education, Sultanate of Oman, Muscat © Ministry of Education, Sultanate of Oman and UNESCO, Paris. Courtesy: UNESCO and Oman Ministry of Education.

1

Introduction: Context, Conference Aims and Organisation

Context

The first article of the 'World Declaration on Education for All' adopted by the World Conference on Education For All held in Jomtien in 1990 asserted that *"every person—child, youth and adult—shall be able to benefit from educational opportunities designed to meet their basic learning needs."* Ten years after Jomtien, the Dakar Framework for Action (UNESCO, 2000, p.8) stated, "Education is a fundamental human right. It is the key to sustainable development and peace and stability within and among countries, and thus an indispensable means for effective participation in the societies and economies of the twenty-first century, which are affected by rapid globalisation."

Out of the six Dakar goals, three had direct implications for the development of Secondary Education. These three goals implied a massive growth of Secondary Education in order to absorb primary school completers, ensure gender parity in enrolment and provide access for all *young people to appropriate learning and life skills. More specifically, the Delors Report exhorted us to see Secondary Education "as a crucial point in the lives of individuals: it is at this stage that young people should be able to decide their own future, in the light of their own tastes and aptitudes, and that they can acquire the abilities that will make for a successful adult life."*

The report continued that Secondary Education "should thus be adapted to take account both of the different processes whereby adolescents attain maturity... and of economic and social needs."

Aware of the fundamental importance of education and the growing need to focus on Secondary Education, the international community has taken up the challenge. Clear commitments have been made within the Dakar framework for action to improve the relevance and effectiveness of Secondary Education. The international conference on secondary education held between December 22 and 24, 2002 in Muscat, was another crucial step on this journey.

Conference Aims and Organisation

In order to complement international efforts and facilitate policy dialogue in respect of this commitment to Secondary Education, The Sultanate of Oman, Ministry of Education International Conference on Reform of Secondary Education—"Secondary Education for a Better Future: Trends, Challenges and Priorities"—aimed to build on both the results of National Seminar on Secondary Education held in Muscat in April, 2002 and the results of the UNESCO International Expert Meeting on General Secondary Education in the 21st Century held in Beijing in May 2001.

The Oman conference received delegates from around 34 countries, contained a total of 77 presentations and was attended by over 400 participants. It was the first time that an international education conference of this magnitude had taken place in the Sultanate and arose because of, as Yahaya bin Saud bin Mansoor Al-Sulaimi, Minister of Education stressed in his opening address, "the importance of exchanging views and experiences with educators so as to enrich the educational system." Secondary Education was described by the Minister as "an important turning point and significant phase in the future of students, and played a key role in economic development and as an engine of social change. Secondary education, in particular, is at a crossroads which can lead in different directions—to specialized and academic higher education, to technical and professional education or directly to the world of work."

Similarly, His Excellency the Director General of UNESCO, Koïchiro Matsuura, in his opening remarks to the conference, pointed out that Secondary Education was of critical importance "in making our future world a better one." He stressed both Secondary Education's impact during the period of adolescence "when important life choices and career orientations for the future are made and its contribution to human resources development as linked with the broader process of social and economic development." However, the Director General of UNESCO was clear in his belief that Secondary Education needs to be redefined if it is to fulfil its assigned functions, that is *"to prepare learners in both formal and non-formal settings for higher education, the world of work and, perhaps most importantly, for responsible citizenship in a changing world."*

In order to continue the international examination of Secondary Education, the Oman conference sought to answer four major questions. These questions were built into five themes treated sequentially over the course of the three days of the conference, each by a keynote speaker and a range of between 10 to 18 referred papers (see the Conference Programme in Annex 3). In addition, the conference was honoured to here from:

- His Excellency Yahaya bin Saud bin Mansoor Al-Sulaimi, Minister of Education
- His Excellency Koïchiro Matsuura, Director General of UNESCO
- Dr Said Al-Mulais, Director General of the Arab Bureau of Education for the Gulf States
- His Excellency Mohammed bin Hamdan Al-Tobi, Under-Secretary for Educational Planning and Projects in the Ministry of Education

- Dr Aziza Banani, Moroccan Ambassador to UNESCO and Chairwoman of the UNESCO Executive Council
- A speech presented by a representative from the Islamic Organisation for Education, Science and Culture (ISESCO)

  (Annex 4 contains the speeches presented at the conference)

The conference themes and topics concentrated on:

- A. Re-defining secondary education for the 21st century: Why change is essential
- B. Effective new models for secondary education in the 21st century: the focus for change
- C. Strategies for successful implementation of reform: practical blueprints for change
- D. Practices in evaluating the success of reform
- E. Sharing new ideas for change

Outline of Report

This report of the Conference is organised around the first four of these five themes (Themes A, B, C, and D). The material from Theme E, sharing new ideas, is not treated as a separate theme but incorporated, as appropriate, into the other four themes. The report is heavily based on theme rapporteur reports (see the Annex 1), which, in turn, are based on issue rapporteur reports and many hours of discussion among issue, session and theme rapporteurs and Ministry of Education and UNESCO representatives.

The report will be clearer in what it has to say about the early themes, that is why and what to change than the later themes. The reason is based on the fact that as one moves through the themes they tend to become more specific. As a theme becomes more specific then *the view taken in this report is that its resolution requires greater consideration of country and local considerations.* This position may be disappointing for some who are looking for 'the answers' but it is consistent with the evidence on successful implementation which shows that those involved in any change need to be fully involved in its development, implementation and assessment—if for no other reason than this involvement results in greater commitment to and acceptance of responsibility for the change. Oman is one country that is clearly on the right track here, for as pointed out by the Ministry of Education, participation in current educational reform efforts has "included all stakeholders—students, parents, teachers, administrators and tertiary education representatives as well as representatives from the private sector and educationalists"

The report undertakes a comparison of outcomes from recent UNESCO reports on Secondary Education from Beijing, Bangkok, Beirut, and Mauritius with the outcomes of both the Oman national and international conferences.

The report also identifies a number of potentially competing theories, beliefs or 'tensions' that became clearer as the conference proceeded. It is argued that while these theories or beliefs are best seen as balances rather than tensions, they will need attention if Secondary Education is to be effectively developed for the 21st century. An example of one of these balances is that between the forces of globalisation and the need to retain a local identity.

The conclusions from Oman/UNESCO conference and the comparison with the results of other reports lead to a number of clear recommendations for reforming Secondary Education. *No recommendation is more important than that Secondary Education should be given higher priority*—for as the World Bank has also concluded, *"education, not physical capital, has become the major source of present and future wealth of nations."*

2

Conference Themes

The conference themes were:

- A. Re-defining secondary education for the 21st century: why change is essential
- B. Effective new models for secondary education in the 21st century: the focus for change
- C. Strategies for successful implementation of reform: practical blueprints for change
- D. Practices in evaluating the success of reform
- E. Sharing new ideas for change

In summary, the conference had the following to say about each of these themes.

Theme A: ***Re-defining Secondary Education for the 21st Century: Why Change is Essential***

Conference papers, presentations and discussions described a rapidly changing world both within and across countries. In particular:

- rapid developments in science, medicine and technology but unevenness in their availability; and,
- wide differences in population growth (for example, in Oman 60 per cent of the total population are under the age of 18).

The result of this rapidly changing world was seen to be increased complexity, for example, from:

- a blurring of boundaries (such as, from the pressures the global marketplace facilitated by developments in information communications technology);
- the end of certainty; and,
- growing inequalities in and across societies (including, as a result of poverty, gender, armed conflict, or even the digital divide).

Major issues raised by this rapid change and increased complexity were seen to include:

- economic competitiveness;
- an economic and labour market where national wealth becomes increasingly knowledge-based and there are changes in the nature of employment;
- sustainability;
- identity within globalisation; and
- equity.

As UNESCO's Director General, Mr. Koïchiro Matsuura, pointed out, the global context sees peace and security threatened in many parts of the world from factors such as civil war, HIV/AIDS, poverty, widespread degradation of renewable resources, illiteracy, and attempts at cultural homogeneity. He goes on to state that, *"Education has a key role to play in making our future world a better one... [and that in] all these areas, Secondary Education has an important contribution to make."*

With universal Primary Education being achieved, Secondary Education was seen by a number of presenters at the conference as the weakest link of education systems, while at the same time it becomes the fastest-expanding sector of formal education. *Secondary Education has become the weakest link not only because of the low enrolment ratio and high dropout rates in some developing nations but also the low relevance, quality and efficiency of programmes, due to factors such as:*

- out-dated information-cramming, discipline-based, college-bound curriculum and an examination-driven evaluation system over-emphasising test scores measuring cognitive achievement and entrance to university;
- passive student/teacher relations rather than ones that promote social construction of knowledge as well as cooperation, problem-solving and critical thinking (for example, in terms of desired generic work skills and/or individual and national identity in an era of globalisation);
- inadequate background (including the qualifications) of many teachers and educational managers;
- over-centralised administration;
- limited stakeholder involvement in education, including from the private sector; and,
- inadequate, inappropriate and uncritical use of the multiple sources of available information, including through the new technology.

These perceived weaknesses of current Secondary Education systems are given even greater attention in a world of increased use and publication of cross-country measures of performance, such as the ongoing OECD Programme for International Student Assessment (PISA). It continues to be important, therefore, to locate national actions and strategies within an international context.

In summary, and risking oversimplification, it is clear that the conference agreed that:

- secondary education should be given higher priority and that commitment to universal access to Secondary Education as an aspiration should be retained;

- change is essential and that the objectives and functions of Secondary Education need to be redefined, renewed and improved to fit with the new realities of the twenty-first century;
- despite the challenges and dilemmas that face Secondary Education now and in the future, reform must continue and build on current strengths and weaknesses; and,
- continued collaboration is required, both nationally and internationally, including in the provision of evidence-based information and examples of innovative best practice.

In brief, and as UNESCO's Director General, Mr Koïchiro Matsuura, pointed out, *"a major, well-coordinated effort must ... be made by national authorities, with the support of international and regional organisations and the active participation of civil society, to meet the long-term objective of universalising quality Secondary Education in the perspective of Education for All."*

Theme B: Effective New Models for Secondary Education in the 21st Century: The Focus for Change

The analysis of context cannot merely consist in identifying overwhelming trends (Theme A) to which we must necessarily submit. Among those trends, educators have to differentiate between what is acceptable and what is not. The conference argued that children are the starting point for a strategy about the future of schooling. A constructive and optimistic vision of their futures and needs should inform the structure and processes of education. However, when the question is asked, 'Does Secondary Education achieve such a vision?' the answer is at best a confused 'perhaps' and at worst 'no'.

UNESCO's DG, Mr Matsuura argued, "the concept of basic education [is] an evolving one: the more the world changes and the more complex societies become, the more sophisticated are the skills needed for social integration and economic participation. This broadens the scope of basic education learned in primary and secondary schools." He added that, "what is currently understood as 'basic education' will be a necessary but insufficient condition. *It can be anticipated that the changes in the twenty-first century will require the expansion, adaptation and improvement of Secondary Education, for the benefit of all.*"

The Delors Report was clear in its recommendation that *"learning in schools needs to focus not just on knowing but also doing, living together and being"*. As secondary schooling is the learning environment in which many young people negotiate their passage through adolescence towards early adulthood, life skills are of particular importance. If schools are not coping with these skills, who else will?

What should be the focus for change in secondary education? The conference papers, presentations and discussions answered this question in a reasonably consistent way. In brief, there was seen to be a need to:

- balance knowledge and cognitive skills with behavioural and life skills (including problem-solving and critical thinking);
- balance vocational and academic education as well as meet the needs of post-Secondary Education;
- raise the awareness of the importance of career guidance;
- increased flexibility and diversity in both content and processes, for example between formal, non-formal and distance education;
- offer students a variety of choices according to their needs, interests and potentials, but in so doing avoid overcrowding the curriculum;
- integrate technology into education; and,
- develop assessment systems that have a balance among reliability, validity, practicability, and compatibility with teaching as well as being centrally and teacher produced.

In terms of curriculum models, it was recommended that *what can be learnt effectively at school may better limited to a set of generic competencies necessary for all work and applicable to a wide range of circumstances.* Such generic competencies have started to appear in recent reviews of education systems. For example, one such review resulted in four new basic clusters for organising the curriculum:

- life pathways and social futures (who am I and where am I going?);
- multiliteracies and communications media (how do I make sense of and communicate with the world?);
- active citizenship (what are my rights and responsibilities in communities, cultures and economies?); and,
- environments and technologies (how do I describe, analyse and shape the world around me?).

Included under the heading of behavioural and life skills, a number of presenters argued persuasively that schools need to participate in the global agenda to transform a culture of peace. The active involvement of youth in the promotion of living together, peace, human rights, sustainable development, and international understanding was seen to need to increase markedly.

Also argued was the need to maintain the dignity of students. Dignity comes from education 'to be'. Yet many curricula and school and teacher practices were seen as marginalising student identity by ignoring their voices and choices. Students, it was argued, must be given the opportunity to express their authentic selves and discover their potentials. In this regard, the whole notion of screening, selection and sifting, especially on a very narrow set of cognitive criteria, may be obsolete. If the scope for cheap labour is continually shrinking, what is the fate of those who have 'failed' in schools? Does it make economic sense for a society to have the majority of its young seeing themselves as failures?

Finally, in terms of building new curriculum models, a particular tension was reported in a number of presentations between pressures exerted by globalisation/ modernity and local identity/traditions. This tension manifest itself, for example, in the balance between pressures exerted by Western modernity and keeping the modest Islamic traditions.

In summary, the conference agreed that in respect of effective models for Secondary Education in the 21st Century:

- countries continue to be committed to the goal of mass, universally accessed Secondary Education;
- there is a recognition that traditionally academically based education and the notion of screening, especially on a very narrow set of cognitive criteria, do not adequately address students' or the society's needs in a context of rapid economic, cultural and social change—schools need to focus and be assessed not just on their contributions to knowing but also to doing, living together and being;
- *life skills are of particular importance—with the active involvement of youth in the promotion of living together, peace, human rights, sustainable development, and international understanding needing to be increased markedly.*
- there is a need to balance vocational/technical and academic education as well as meet the needs of post-Secondary Education;
- education systems and schools need to increase flexibility, responsiveness and diversity in both content and processes—offering students a variety of choices according to their needs, interests and potentials—but at the same time not overcrowd the curriculum; and,

- there is a need in all that we do to maintain student dignity.

Theme C: Strategies for Successful Implementation of Reform: Practical Blueprints for Change

How to change (the priorities or strategies for effective implementation) was the topic of Theme C. In summary, strategies for successful implementation of reform were seen to rest on at least five pillars:

- student involvement, as well as taking account of students and their needs;
- teacher involvement, and quality of pre and ongoing in-service teacher education (and selection for);
- quality leadership, and its development and renewal;
- family and community involvement, and development (social capital); and,
- private and public sector involvement, particularly in addressing labour market demands. In fact, what was suggested was a multi-sectoral approach enlisting the collective efforts of government and their ministries, NGOs, local communities, the private sector, etc.

Implicit in this vision for wide stakeholder involvement in educational reform is that successful implementation:

- favours a move from centralised to decentralised school and system management, including greater use of networking;
- takes time;
- is developmental in nature; and,
- needs to recognise that people (students, teachers, principals) develop knowledge and skills on a continuing basis (lifelong learning).

Theme *B* (the focus for change) has already stressed the importance of students, of taking account of them and their needs, particularly in the behavioural and life skill areas. Theme *B* also stressed the importance of maintaining student dignity. Theme C conference papers, presentations and discussions argued for greater student involvement in school curriculum and administration. Through this involvement students were seen to need to be able to develop the confidence.

To attempt to bring about major change without carrying along teachers was seen as very unwise. Compliance without commitment, it was argued, does not bring about successful long-term implementation. Reform of schooling, no matter how well conceptualised, powerfully sponsored, or closely audited will often fail in the face of resistance (or inaction) from teachers. Teacher shortages were seen as compounding any implementation difficulties. *Given the importance of teachers in a strategy of successful implementation of reform, the quality of the criteria for their selection and their pre and in-service education become especially important as areas requiring attention.*

School leaders, including principals, were also seen as critically important in achieving school effectiveness and improvement and, as reforms designed to raise standards are introduced (for example, decentralisation and school-based-management and/or community involvement), their roles change significantly.

It was argued that a new kind of educational leader is required and that policy makers should be compelled to develop and modify their national training strategies to equip school leaders with the knowledge and skills required to carry out these changed roles.

Reframing schools as learning organisations, where the structures, processes and practices foster continuous learning of all those involved, is rapidly gaining favour in both the arenas of research and policy. The concept of schools as learning organisations has grown out of the need to create school environments where all are learning how to learn together. This development reinforces the need to distinguish between leadership as a function which all can do (that is, distributive leadership) and leadership as a role which is held by the position holder, such as the principal.

But school settings are not necessarily conducive to such learning, especially where it extends beyond the school to family and community involvement and development. This situation is unfortunate, especially given the strong link between such factors as home educational environment and school climate and results—a stronger link in some countries than socio-economic status. School councils representing all parties comprising a community with active encouragement to attend and involvement in meaningful activities was seen as one strategy for greater family and community involvement and development. On the other hand, it was recommended that *more students be given opportunities to be involved in such councils as well as in community service.*

Private and public sector institutions were seen as playing an important role in strategies for successful implementation of reform.

This involvement could take a number of forms including support for infrastructure, specific projects, sponsorship, and curriculum initiatives. These private and public institutions could profitably be involved in strengthening the linkage between schools and the world of work through vocational guidance, study-work alternation and clarification of changing labour market requirements.

The general consensus, after many years of educational reform initiatives, was that too little changes too slowly. This situation is particularly so in a context where too much is implemented too quickly. Permeating all the recommendations on how to change was the position that stragies for effective implementation favour decentralised management, take time, are developmental in nature, and need to recognise that people (students, teachers, principals) develop knowledge and skills on a continuing basis (lifelong learning).

For example, research on schools as learning organisations has shown clearly that one needs to first get the personal/interpersonal, distributive leadership, collective teacher efficacy or trusting and collaborative climate 'right'. Once the personal/interpersonal is 'right' then it can be used to focus on the educational/instructional, including having a shared and monitored mission. Once the educational/instructional is 'right' and there is confidence in what the school is doing and why it is doing it, then the leaders and school can move to development/learning/change, to taking initiatives and risks, including for example working with others schools in a 'nested' model.

Development implies another important principle—one needs stability for change, one needs to constantly move ahead but without losing one's roots. Put another way, one needs a base or agreed position from which to develop; one needs to stand for something, to first be 'grounded'. In targeting strategies or interventions to help this development recognition needs to be given to the fact that actions at one stage may be inappropriate, or even counterproductive, at another stage. Achieving balanced learning/development may, in fact, mean that a school system or individual school recognises and understands such stages and can take the appropriate action without being 'bowled over' by the change that surrounds it. It may mean understanding (to jump briefly to Theme D) that schools will be evaluated differently depending on the stage it has reached. It also, eventually, involves those in education systems and schools being risk takers.

Theme D: Practices in Evaluating the Success of Reform

Theme *D* focused on how do we know we've been successful, or the practices we might use in evaluating the success of reform. Topics considered by the conference in answering this question centred on:

- accountability;
- maximising access, opportunity and completion rates;
- measuring improvement in educational outcomes; and
- Examining indicators of capacity building at the school and community level.

Accountability in education is a contested and complex concept. Despite this, some form of accountability is as inevitable as it is important. Given the growing understanding of the crucial importance of education for the future prosperity of their countries (see Theme *A*), it was reported that governments are looking for ways to exercising central control over schools. Part of the logic for these developments is linked to exposing education to the market.

Despite these national developments in educational accountability, there are those, usually from outside national governments and their ministries, who urge caution. There are contested areas and they seem to centre on questions such as why accountability is being undertaken (for example, for central control, resource distribution and/or local school improvement) and who and what is involved (for example, the employer, professionals, parents, and/or students and central and/or local curriculum, standards, inspection, testing).

It might be that centrally-defined output criteria and local innovation in finding ways of meeting them are not necessarily contradictory; what matters is the degree to which specification of standards becomes so detailed and interventionist that a culture of control rather than autonomy develops. It was reported, for example, that the establishment of student standards, wide-spread student testing of their achievement and judgements about schools and teachers based on the results can have disasterous unintended consequences. For students, such consequences may include, minimising their individual differences, narrowing curriculum to which they are exposed, diverting enormous efforts from instruction to test preparation, and negatively influencing schools' willingness to accept students with weak academic records. The consequences for teachers may include the creation of incentives for cheating, feelings of shame, guilt and anger, and a sense of dissonance and alienation and to the atrophy of teachers' instructional repertoires.

Accountability pressures are not only national in nature. At the international level UNESCO's Monitoring Learning Achievement (MLA) project and OECD's PISA are having an impact on national educational policy. Given the cautions about some developments in educational accountability, what was thought encouraging about this international work was its taking into account such factors as the socio-economic status and home educational environment of the student, the school learning environment and a broad range of educational outcomes, including not only different literacies but also student life skills and engagement in their education.

The degree of inclusion practised in different education systems, in terms of factors such as maximising access, opportunity and completion rates, was found to vary quite widely—from including only those with special education needs to any group which might be marginalised, whether these be girls or boys, ethnic minorities an/or the gifted and talented. There was felt to be a need, for example, to raise the awareness the social, economic and development cost of neglecting the education of girls and establishing sound indicators to monitor and evaluate technical and vocational tracks offered for them. But it was agreed that there was still much to do in making schools more inclusive, including providing appropriate training for teachers, materials and equipment. Pleas were made for more time to make the required changes and more forums for exchange of experiences.

While the final aim of a school-reform evaluator must be to discover if a reform programme has led to improved educational quality, an important along-the-way choice faces those measuring improvement—do they take a 'hands-off' appraisal or, instead, take a more proactive role in nurturing improvement? Given that research and experience have shown that the tests of students' performance are immensely influential on the instruction that transpires as part of any reform initiative, it was argued that it is incumbent on the school-reform evaluator to first installs instructionally supportive tests as their dominant data-gathering device.

A major highlight in Theme *D* was *a call to broaden what counts for effective education beyond academic achievement to what could be termed 'capacity building'*. For example, very interesting data was reported from a British cohort study found that attentiveness in school at age 10 years was a key aspect of human capital production at age 26, also influencing female wages even taking into account qualifications. Boys with high levels of conduct disorder were much more likely to experience unemployment. High self-esteem was found to both reduce the likelihood of that unemployment lasting more than a year and, for all males, increase wages. Locus of control was an important predictor of female wages. Good peer relations were found to reduce the probability of unemployment and increasing female wages. These findings, as well as the arguments presented earlier in respect of the crucial importance of learning to learn, cooperation, problem-solving, critical thinking, and so on, add weight to those expressing concerns about the sole reliance on academic, cognitive achievement to measure success.

In summary, practices for evaluating the success of reform should understand that:

- care needs to be taken that the degree of standards specification does not become so detailed and interventionist that a culture of control rather than autonomy develops;
- there is a need to raise the awareness the social, economic and development costs of weak inclusion policies, including a neglect of girls education;

- school-reform evaluators need to first install instructionally supportive tests as their dominant data-gathering device;
- measuring educational success has to take into account such contextual factors as the socio-economic status and home educational environment of the student and the school learning environment; and,
- measuring educational success has to rely on more than academic, cognitive achievement.

3

Comparison of Outcomes from UNESCO Reports from Beijing, Beirut, Bangkok, and Mauritius with the Outcomes of the Muscat National and International Conferences

A comparison of outcomes from recent UNESCO reports from meetings in Beijing, Bangkok, Beirut, and Mauritius with the outcomes of the Sultanate of Oman national and international conferences on Secondary Education, contained in the following chart, leave the one with a number of very clear impressions:

- agreement that education has a key role to play in making our future world a better one;
- consistency advice on why, what and how to change Secondary Education to achieve this better world;
- the need for greater national and international priority to be given to Secondary Education;
- the need not just for Secondary Education to be expanded but also for its objectives and functions to be redefined, renewed and improved; and,

- a continuing role for international bodies such as UNESCO in facilitating dialogue and providing evidence-based information about this redefinition, renewal and improvement.

In the chart that follows, a summary of the results from the conference is used (left hand column) as the basis of comparison with the other reports. If an additional recommendation is identified it is added in the column representing that report. A summary of the outcomes of each of these reports can be found in the Annex. The reports consulted are as follows:

UNESCO, (2001) Executive summary: Meeting agreements. *International expert meeting on general Secondary Education in the Twenty-first Century: Trends, challenges and priorities.* Paris: UNESCO Final Report on the meeting held in Beijing, People's Republic of China, May 21-25, pp. 5-8.

Billeh, V., BouJaoude, S., & Sulieman, S. (2002). *Regional Synthesis on Development of Secondary Education in the Arab States.* Beirut: UNESCO Regional Office.

Zhou Nan-zhao & Haw, G. (2002). *Secondary Education Reforms in Asia-Pacific Region: Challenges, Strategies and Programme Actions in Addressing Learners' Needs.* A report on the 8th UNESCO-APEID International Conference in Education held in Bangkok 26-29 November, 2002 and presented as a paper at Sultanate of Oman Ministry of Education/UNESCO International Conference Secondary Education for a Bettern Future: Trends, Challenges and Priorities, Muscat, Sultanate of Oman, 22-24 December. (2002). pp. 19-22.

UNESCO Dakar Regional Office. (2002). *General Report of the Regional Workshop on the Reform of Secondary Education in Africa.* Mauritius, 3-6 December, 2002.

Sultanate of Oman/Ministry of Education. *Recommendations of the National Seminar on Secondary Education. Muscat, 1-3 April 2002.*

Comparison of Outcomes from UNESCO Reports and Oman

Muscat		*Beijing*	*Beirut*	*Mauritius*	*Bangkok*	*Muscat*
Oman/UNESCO		*UNESCO*	*UNESCO*	*UNESCO*	*UNESCO*	*OMAN*
01/12/2002		*May 02*	*December 02*	*December 02*	*November 02*	*April 02*
1.	**Why Change?**					
1.1	**Secondary Education should be given higher priority and that commitment to universal access to Secondary Education as an aspiration should be retained;**	X	I	I	X	I
1.2	**Change is essential and that the objectives and functions of Secondary Education need to be redefined, renewed and improved to fit with the new realities of the twenty-first century;**	X	I	I	X	I
1.3	**Despite the challenges and dilemmas that face secondary education now and in the future, reform must continue and build on current strengths and weaknesses; and,**	X		X	I	I
1.4	**1.4 continued collaboration is required, both nationally and internationally, including in the provision of evidence-based information and examples of innovative best practice.**	X	X	X	X	X
		I			Major review (like Jomtien)	

(Contd.)

(Contd.)

2.	**What change?**					
2.1	Countries continue to be committed to the goal of mass, universally accessed Secondary Education;	X		I	I	I
2.2	There is a recognition that traditionally academically based education and the notion of screening, especially on a very narrow set of cognitive criteria, do not adequately address students? or the society's needs in a context of rapid economic, cultural and social change-schools need to focus and be assessed not just on their contributions to knowing but also to doing, living together and being;	X	X	X	X	X
2.3	Life skills are of particular importance—with the active involvement of youth in the promotion of living together, peace, human rights, sustainable development, and international understanding needing to be increased markedly;	X		X	X	X
2.4	There is a need to balance vocational/technical and academic education as well as meet the needs of post-Secondary Education;	X	X	X	X	X
2.5	Education systems and schools need to increase flexibility, resposiveness and diversity in both content and processes—offering students a variety of choices according to their needs, interests and potentials—but at the same time not overcrowd the curriculum; and,	X	X	X	X	X

(Contd.)

2.6	There is a need in all that we do to maintain student dignity.	I		I	X	I
		X		X	Creative use of ICT	X
						Islamic ideology & Oman cultural identity will be the base for reform
						Increasing learning time in school day & year
3.	**How Change?**					
3.1	Student involvement, as well as taking account of students and their needs;	X	X	X	X	I
3.2	Teacher involvement, and quality pre and on going in-service teacher education (including selection for);	X	X	X	X	X

(Contd.)

(Contd.)

3.3	Quality leadership, and its development and renewal;	X		X		X
				Including capacity building		
3.4	Family and community involvement, and development (social capital);	X	X	X	X	I
3.5	Private and public sector involvement, particularly in addressing labour market demands. In fact, what is suggested is a multi-sectoral approach enlisting the collective efforts of government and their ministries, NGOs, local communities, the private sector, etc;	X	X	X	X	X
3.6	Move from centralised to decentalised school and system management including greater participation of all stakeholders and use of networking;	X	X	X	X	X
3.7	Take time;					
3.8	See change as developmental in nature; and,			I		
3.9	Recognise that people (students, teachers, principals) develop knowledge and skills on a continuing basis (lifelong learning).	X	X	I		
		Student should be the centre of reform		X		

(Contd.)

			Adequate infrastructure situated close to clients	Decrease emphasis on text books
				Establish regional teacher training centres
4.	How do we know we've been successful?			
4.1	Care needs to be taken that the degree of standards specification does not become so detailed and interventionist that a culture of control rather than autonomy develops;		X	
4.2	There is a need to raise the awareness the social, economic and development cost of weak inclusion policies, including a neglect of girls' education;	X	I	
4.3	School-reform evaluators need to first install instructionally supportive tests as their dominant data-gathering device;		X	I
4.4	Measuring educational success has to take into account such contextual factors as the socio-economic status and home educational environment of the student and the school learning environment; and,	I	I	

(Contd.)

(Contd.)

4.5	Measuring educational success has to rely on more than academic, cognitive achievement.	X		I	X	X
				X And use for quality control in a decentralised system	Develope core quality indicators	
		X		X	School physical & psychological health	X
		X		X	Government priority in planning	X
				X		Use continuous evaluation
						Establish and education and assessment centre

KeyX= Agreement I= Implied Agreement

4

The Need for Balance*

An overview of the different papers and the results of the various discussion sessions of the conference suggests that there was a consensus among most countries and speakers that Secondary Education is and will remain the responsibility of all stakeholders in any society and that issues surrounding Secondary Education vary according to the various social contexts but that it will need to be reformed to meet the demands of a better future.

At a macro level, the interests of each stakeholder could result in major differences in beliefs about the definition and purpose of, and the changes needed in, Secondary Education. However, as a result of better understanding ongoing social, political and cultural changes within countries and around the world, the conference emphasized the importance of achieving balance between these interests, beliefs or 'tensions'. It is, in fact, proposed that we examine these interests or beliefs as balances rather than tensions. Focusing on different interests, beliefs or tensions might imply that we are only dealing with mutually exclusive options.

---

* The assistance of Dr Said al Kitani, the other conference General Rapporteur and Director of the Sultanate of Oman, Minister of Education's Office, in developing and writing this section is acknowledged, although its final form is the sole responsibility of the author.

A reexamination of the results of the conference across the four Themes helps identify a number of balances.[1] This section of the conference report provides a brief account of twelve balances—balances that, while not without overlap, might need to be 'balanced' in each education system within the general framework of developing world class Secondary Education for a better future. These balances are between:

- continuity and change;
- dependence and independence;
- individual and community;
- homogeneity and heterogeneity;
- spiritual and material
- global and local;
- education for education and education for work as well as academic and life skills;
- competition and cooperation;
- knowledge-experience explosion and human capacity;
- uncertainty and future scenarios;
- process and outcomes; and,
- social institution's expectations and educator's practices.

Continuity and Constant Change

In contrast to past continuity, recent times have witnessed constant change, a stream of new movements, new programmes and new directions. Unfortunately, conference papers give the impression that some in education seem to be forever rushing to catch the next bandwagon that hits the scene. 'Unfortunately' because there is increasing evidence that some schools and school systems have been badly disillusioned by the galloping hoof beats of the itinerant peddlers behind the new movements who ride in and out again extorting their latest elixir.

The core paradox in a such a situation, a world of massive and constant change, seems to be how to foster enough internal stability in people and the organisation in which they work in order to encourage the pursuit of change. *Stability for change, moving ahead without losing our roots, is the challenge.* Another way of putting this would be to assert that the most successful secondary schools of the new age will be those that are able to balance the market pressures of adaptation and dynamism with social concerns of security and dignity.

It might be helpful in this situation for us to remember Noah's principle: one survives not by predicting rain but by building arks. As some of the conference papers demonstrated, amid uncertain, continually changing conditions, leading educational leaders are constructing arks comprising their collective capacity to learn, they are striving to become intelligent, or learning, organisations.

Dependence and Independence

A second fundamental issue relates to the balance between dependence and independence. This situation is most easily seen conference papers implying an over dependence by those in educational institutions on 'leaders', often engendered by the overconfidence of 'leaders' in their own abilities or importance. There seem to be a lot of people around these days who want to tell those in schools what to do. This situation is unfortunate. It is unfortunate because some of those doing the telling do not always accept responsibility for their advice, are not around long enough to take responsibility for their directions and to may even seek to prevent fair and open assessment of the changes they promulgate. It is also unfortunate because while those in schools cannot avoid change they are the people who have to implement change. As some of the conference papers argued, those in schools need to have more to say about what is happening in our world, what it means for our schools and how it will be implemented and assessed—in other words, they need more independence.

Individualism and Community

It may be unreasonable to expect the schools to pick up the slack when, as described in different conference papers, families fall apart, religious institutions no longer attract the young, children are malnourished, drug addiction is rampant, prime-time television programmes are vacuous and educationally bankrupt, and gang members, athletes, and narcissistic celebrities are the admired adolescent role models. However, *if the home and school do not pick up the responsibility for our young then who will?*

Who will counter, for example, the pressure inherent in much of our 'modern' society to act alone rather than with, or for, the community? *An elementary level of trust necessary is for community. Where is such trust established, if not in our homes and schools?* Turning back the tide of a 'virtual' world, with its stress on individualism and encouragement to dissociate oneself from an increasingly challenging world, is vital for the future survival of our societies. *Community is a place where conflict can be resolved without physical or emotional bloodshed. It could be said that a community is a group that can 'fight gracefully'.*

Homogeneity and Heterogeneity

If you look for common denominators in successful institutions, it was argued that a strong one is to find a way to get some of the people to do a deviant thing, to take the initiative, to take risks. If a system is too tight for this there will be no search and no development. Also, as some conference papers pointed out, *the worker sought in the future will be one who thinks, questions, innovates and takes entrepreneurial risk, as well as one that can work in regularly changing teams.*

One lesson here is that reductionist approaches in education, to the complexity that is the world of the teacher and the student, should not go unchallenged. As a number of conference papers pointed out, uniformity for education systems in aims, in standards, and in methods of assessment is a complexity-reducing mechanism. *It is far tidier to have a single set of aims for all, a single curriculum for all, a single set of standards for all, and a single array of tests for all than to have locally developed approaches to school improvement.* However, homogeneity of outcome for the future of our society is not necessarily the highest good, and may be impossible to achieve. On the other hand, recognising diversity and acknowledging the multiple ways to be and act can be seen as a potential source of strength to a culture.

Spiritual and Material

As pointed to by the Director-General of the UNESCO during the conference opening ceremony "peace and security are threatened in many parts of the world and many countries are living in situations of crisis and conflict. Civil wars are a key source of human suffering in today's world, where billions of dollars are spent on weapons". In addition it was reported at the conference that poverty and diseases such as HIV/AIDS continues to affect millions of people, especially young people, around the world. Similarly, WHO in its recent world report on violence and health states that today no country or community is untouched by violence. Images and accounts of violence pervade the media; it is on our streets, in our homes, schools, workplaces and institutions. Violence is a universal scourge that tears at the fabric of communities and threatens the life, health and happiness of all of us. Each year, more than 1.6 million people worldwide lose their lives to violence.

These horrifying facts about violence may be partly a result of the imbalance between the spiritual and the material dimensions of the human life. Therefore, it is not surprising to find a call in the conference for serious consideration of balancing human spiritual aspects and the technical productivity-based aspects in developing Secondary Education for a better future. This balance is also clearly expressed in the first of 39 recommendations from the Oman National seminar on Secondary Education held in Muscat in April, 2002: "Islamic ideology, values of the society and the Omani cultural identity shall be the base for the reform of Education in the Sultanate of Oman."

Global and Local

With the revolution of technology and telecommunications, globalisation in its various forms is a fact of today's and future life. As some conference papers argued, this does not necessarily mean the domination of one particular culture over another; rather it means people around the world being able within their respective cultures to enjoy the privilege of living together in the global village. It was seen that for this to happen a balance needed to be achieved in Secondary Education between *emphasizing the role of students as citizens of their respective countries and their role as global citizens*. Related to this position was the notion of keeping balance between responding to modernity and preserving national identities.

Education for Education and Education for Work as Well as Academic and Life Skills

Debate on education for its own sake or for work continued at the conference. Conference papers confirmed that *ignorance and social breakdown are not less serious than unemployment and coping with the rapidly changing job markets of the world*. Both need to be addressed. Thus, an over-emphasis on academic based education such as found in science and technology-based subjects at the expense of humanities and life-skills in secondary schools would create imbalance. The conference, in fact, concluded that *life skills are of particular importance with the active involvement of youth in the promotion of living together, peace, human rights, sustainable development, and international understanding needing to be markedly increased in secondary schools.*

Competition and Cooperation

It was reported at the conference that competitiveness permeates many education systems around the world.

Nations attempt to develop human resources that are capable of competing with other nations, communities, organisations and people in various fields on life. However, nations, communities, organisations and people also cooperate and work together in order to achieve better futures. *Organisations and commercial and industrial firms, for example, are increasingly moving towards coordinating their businesses. This situation puts Secondary Education in the forefront of the challenge of educating students in both how to compete and how to cooperate.* Balance between these two concepts becomes increasingly essential in today's world.

Knowledge-experience Explosion and Human Capacity

It was reported at the conference that the quantity of the information is increasing at a staggering rate, in part due to the sheer amount of computing power available, and in part to the general explosion of knowledge and research. Thousands of publications are published daily around the world in various fields of life that report knowledge needing to be available to Secondary Education students. However, it was also argued that schools neither have time and ability during schooling years to transfer all that information to *students nor have social responsibility for doing so. Instead, some conference papers argued that students need to be taught processes for dealing with and to handle the steadily increasing amount of information and experiences to which they are exposed through the various types of media.*

The conference highlighted the significance of maintaining balance between, on one hand, the amount and the depth of information included in Secondary Education curriculum and, on the other hand, the strategies, skills and techniques that are likely to help students handle information and deal with it effectively and efficiently.

Uncertainty and Future Scenarios

Conference papers described Secondary Education today as being developed in a world increasingly characterized by great uncertainties—uncertainties associated with rapid economic, technological, political and social changes. When change accelerates, it becomes very difficult to anticipate what will occur. Some experts suggest that change has so accelerated that long-range planning is no longer possible. At the same time, participants of the conference pointed to the fact that there is a fashionable trend nowadays to develop scenarios for the future. Educational systems attempt to develop curricula that are directed towards one of those scenarios, whether at micro or macro level. However, because of the unpredictable nature of social change there are no guarantees that the future will be as perceived in those scenarios. *It is, therefore, important to maintain balance between future expectations and curricula design through ensuring a degree of flexibility, which can make curricula constantly adaptable to changing circumstances.*

Process and Outcome

Some conference papers argue that the general direction of the debate over Secondary Education is dominated by an exaggerated emphasis on the outcomes of secondary schools without an equal emphasis placed upon the processes of preparing those outcomes. It was suggested that this imbalance is a direct result of the overwhelming market place debate that has been going on since the 1970s. Societies (governments, politicians, parents, and even students) are concerned about what kind of skills and competencies young people will have when they graduate from secondary schools. While this concern has to be taken into account, conference papers also pointed out that it is important to be concern about the quality of processes that are responsible for creating and shaping secondary school students during the schooling years. These processes include such issues as curricula design, pedagogy, learning strategies, assessment strategies, and so on. *Balance is needed then between the development of our understanding of the kind of school graduates we need and the development of the quality of processes needed for arriving at those graduates.*

Social Institutions' Expectations and Educators' Practices

Conference papers revealed that various social institutions such as family and job market have certain expectations of secondary schools graduates. Nevertheless, educators' practices in schools are not always seen to be consistent with those expectations. As a result, poor school-home and school-job market relationships are reported.

This is neither to argue for family and job market, nor to argue for educators, and their practices. Rather, it is to argue that effective and productive communication is needed between the various social institutions on one hand, and educators on the other. Students spend a small proportion of their time in schools and the rest outside school. *It was argued that students do better in schools when they have strong home educational environments* (including getting effective instructions from their families about how they should organize their learning time, develop plans, and create visions about their school and life generally). Thus, it is crucial to maintain balance between what social institutions expect of students and how educators conduct teaching and learning in secondary schools.

NOTE

1. This approach has been taken elsewhere, for example: "Consider a balance: in the pan on our right we see piled the so-called 'modern' values of contracts, markets and competition; the instrumental skills of efficiency, accountability, planning; a focus on the short-term, the symbolic and expedient; having the answers; sameness; doing things right. It is fair then to ask whether in the pan on our left we have enough of the perhaps more 'old-fashioned' values of wisdom, trust, empathy, compassion, grace, honesty; the skills of collaboration and reciprocity; a focus on the long-term, the real and substantive; discretion and reserving judgment; character; doing the right thing." (p. 123) (From: Mulford, B. 2002. The Global Challenge: A Matter of Balance. Educational Management & Administration. 30 (2), 123-138.)

5

Conclusion: Recommendations for Reforming Secondary Education

The Oman Ministry of Education/UNESCO International Conference on the Reform of Secondary Education, "Secondary Education for a Better Future—Trends, Challenges and Priorities", results in the following recommendations for reforming Secondary Education (recommendations marked with an asterisk are taken from material reviewed for this report from other UNESCO or Omani reports and Annex 2). Recommendations are organised by conference Themes.

1. Re-defining Secondary Education for the 21st Century: Why Change is Essential

1. Secondary Education should be given higher priority and that commitment to universal access to Secondary Education as an aspiration should be retained;
2. change is essential and that the objectives and functions of Secondary Education need to be redefined, renewed and improved to fit with the new realities of the twenty-first century;
3. despite the challenges and dilemmas that face secondary education now and in the future, reform must continue and build on current strengths and weaknesses;

4. continued collaboration is required, both nationally and internationally, including in the provision of evidence-based information and examples of innovative best practice; and,

*5. UNESCO undertakes a major review of Secondary Education (like jomtien).

2. ***Effective New Models for Secondary Education in the 21st Century: The Focus for Change***

1. countries continue to be committed to the goal of mass, universally accessed Secondary Education;

2. the beliefs and values of the society and cultural identity need to form the base for any reform;

3. there is a recognition that traditionally academically based education and the notion of screening, especially on a very narrow set of cognitive criteria, do not adequately address students' or the society's needs in a context of rapid economic, cultural and social change—schools need to focus and be assessed not just on their contributions to knowing but also to doing, living together and being;

4. life skills are of particular importance—with the active involvement of youth in the promotion of living together, peace, human rights, sustainable development, and international understanding needing to be increased markedly;

5. there is a need to balance vocational/technical and academic education as well as meet the needs of post-Secondary Education;

6. education systems and schools need to increase flexibility, responsiveness and diversity in both content and processes—offering students a variety of choices according to their needs, interests and potentials—but at the same time not overcrowd the curriculum (*and decrease emphasis on textbooks);

7. there is a need in all that we do to maintain student dignity; and,
8. there is a need to better integrate and make more creative use of ICT.

3. *Strategies for Successful Implementation of Reform: Practical Blueprints for Change*

1. student involvement, as well as taking account of students and their needs (students need to be the centre of any reform);
2. teacher involvement, and quality pre and ongoing in-service teacher education (and selection for);
3. quality leadership, and its development and renewal;
4. family and community involvement, and development (that is, social capital development);
5. private and public sector involvement, particularly in addressing labour market demands—in fact, what is suggested is a multi-sectoral approach enlisting the collective efforts of government and their ministries, NGOs, local communities, the private sector, etc;
6. move from centralised to decentralised school and system management, including greater participation of all stakeholders and use of networking;
7. take time;
8. see change as developmental in nature;
9. recognise and act on the understanding that people (students, teachers, principals) develop knowledge and skills on a continuing basis (lifelong learning); and,
10. recognise and act on the understanding that effective change will need to involve achieving a balance between:

(i) continuity and change;

(ii) dependence and independence;

(iii) individual and community;

(iv) homogeneity and heterogeneity;

(v) spiritual and material;

(vi) global and local;

(vii) education for education and education for work as well as academic and life skills;

(viii) competition and cooperation;

(ix) knowledge-experience explosion and human capacity;

(x) uncertainty and future scenarios;

(xi) process and outcomes; and,

(xii) social institution's expectations and educator's practices.

4. *Practices in Evaluating the Success of Reform*

1. the level of UNESCO and Government priority in planning and resource distribution for Secondary Education;

2. develop and use core quality indicators (including of school physical and psychological health).

3. in measuring success a number of factors need to be taken into account, including:

   (i) measuring educational success has to rely on more than academic, cognitive achievement;

   (ii) school-reform evaluators need to first install instructionally supportive tests as their dominant data-gathering device;

   (iii) care needs to be taken that the degree of standards specification does not become

so detailed and interventionist that a culture of control rather than autonomy develops;

(iv) measuring educational success has to take into account such contextual factors as the socio-economic status and home educational environment of the student and the school learning environment; and,

(v) the need to raise the awareness the social, economic and development cost of weak inclusion policies, including a neglect of girls' education.

ANNEXES

I. Conference Theme Rapporteur Reports

The conference was built on five themes:

- A. Re-defining secondary education for the 21st century: why change is essential
- B. Effective new models for secondary education in the 21st century: the focus for change
- C. Strategies for successful implementation of reform: practical blueprints for change
- D. Practices in evaluating the success of reform
- E. Sharing new ideas for change

Rapporteur reports on each of these themes follow:

Theme A: Re-defining Secondary Education for the 21st Century: Why Change is Essential

Dr. Abdullah bin Khamis Ambusaidi

College of Education at Sultan Qaboos University

Number of Papers Presented: 12

Keynote Speaker: HE Koïchiro Matsuura, Director-General, UNESCO

Topics:

Topic A.1: Aligning the objectives and functions of secondary education to meet the new realities of the 21st century.

Topic A.2: Major challenges and dilemmas that face secondary education now and in the future, and the role of reform in meetings these challenges and dilemmas.

Topic A.3: Building on strengths and overcoming weaknesses: Priority areas for reform.

Introduction

Secondary education is playing a vital role in any educational system that is due to the key position of this level between primary education and higher education. Therefore, specifying the objectives and functions of secondary education becomes important for every country throughout the world. Furthermore, we are now living in a century which has a lot of rapid changes economically, technology and socially. These changes are facing secondary education internationally, including in developing countries and in Arab countries.

The Challenges Facing Secondary Education in the 21st Century Internationally

There are many challenges and dilemmas associated with the 21st century. It is not the place to go through them in detail but to summarize them and their implications for secondary education. The challenges arise because of factors such as globalisation, technology, society, the economy and workplace, and issues of security, disease and growing gaps among countries.

1. *Globalisation*

This might be the biggest challenge facing the secondary education. Globalisation does not have only economy boundaries, but it has also cultural and political side effects. Consequently, how we can get benefits of this phenomenon without affecting the culture of the society? Furthermore, how we are going to prepare our students in secondary education to deal successfully with both the positive and negative effects of such a phenomenon?

The implications for secondary education include:

- Each educational system should help its students recognise their identities in this era of globalisation. For example, one recommendation of the National Seminar on Secondary Education held in Muscat-sultanate of Oman (1/4-3/4/02) states "Islamic ideology, values of the society and the Omani cultural identity shall be the base for the reform of Education in the Sultanate of Oman".
- Teachers should be trained not only in teaching students the academic subjects but also guide and teach these students to deal with the international challenges of 21st century.

2. *Technology*

This challenge is related or linked to the first challenge. The obvious aspect of this challenge is the Internet. Internet provides a lot of information but the crucial question here is whether or not to accept or reject everything uncritically. We need to train our students to deal with the Internet in a proper way. The major source of information is no longer schools. There are other sources such as the media. It is real challenge to secondary education to be critical consumers of what is coming from the media.

The educational implications include:

- As we cannot avoid the rapid movement of information in the era of technology and globalization, information communication technology (ICT) should be used as one of the bases of any reform in secondary education.

- ICT should be considered as one of the core subjects in the curriculum, or at least integrated with other courses.
- Teachers should be trained to deal with the new technology, otherwise they may find themselves falling behind their students.
- The new technology in schools needs to be continuously supported financially. The government and private sectors should work together to fulfill this aim.
- Media can play an important role in assisting the development of secondary education reform.

3. *Society*

Society is changing rapidly. For example, in some countries, there are some jobs that were not available to women ten years ago but today they are for both genders, for example, nursing. Some argue that technology is helping make society more sophisticated. Furthermore, it is noted that the social bonds between people in the society are changing; particularly in urban areas.

The educational implications include:

- There should be priority given to human and social factors in an educated society. To achieve this there is a need to shift from the passive culture of students/teachers relationship to active and dynamics relationships which promote critical thinking and cooperation.
- The view of school needs to change to emphasize social and learning communities rather than mere academic study.
- The wider community should be more involved in setting educational policy, for example for student discipline.

4. *Economy and Workplace*

One of the major changes in the economy is the movement from being industrial to the knowledge based. Furthermore, fanned by globalisationthere is high degree of competition in the today's economy. Consequently, the nature of workplace is also changing. Today, the workplace asks for people with higher professional qualifications and skills. Unskilled people have less and less place. A work force, which is able to adapt itself to new areas of real situations, is more needed in today's market than one that has theoretical knowledge only.

The educational implications include:

- Students should have the ability to communicate, work in teams, adapt to change, to be innovative and creative, and be familiar with the new technology.
- There is a need to concentrate more on the behavioural outcomes of secondary education than the cognitive.
- As secondary education is an important time in which adolescents discover their abilities and interests, it is important that counseling, guidance and careers guidance processes take place.
- The private sector should be encouraged to play a very important role in secondary education reform, especially in the curriculum.

5. *Other Challenges*

There are other challenges, such as:

- The lack of peace and security in many countries that leaves them without stability.
- Diseases such as HIV/AIDS, which kill many people very year, especially in developing countries.
- The increasing gap between developed and developing countries.

The educational implications of these other challenges include:

- Students should be aware of the importance of peace and security. The school curriculum needs to emphasize this issue in its content.
- Students should be made aware of the danger of issues surrounding epidemic diseases such as HIV/AIDS so that they can help prevent them.

Two Challenges Facing Secondary Education in the 21st Century in Developing and Arab Countries

Now I move to talk about status of the secondary education in the developing countries in general and Arab countries, in particular the graduates and the curriculum.

1. Graduates

The graduates in secondary education currently have few skills to enter the world of work. Although, there are two streams of secondary education in some countries, academic and vocational, nether of them seems capable of achieving the requirements of the world of work. Also, those who are going to be enrolled in higher education are not seen well prepared. Higher education requires students to do more than memorizing facts and principles. It requires them to solve problems, do projects, analyze data, and set up hypothesizes and test them.

2. Curriculum

There is a growing irrelevance of the school curriculum to students' own lives and future careers. This situation contributes to negative students' attitudes towards school and some courses, such as science and mathematics. Secondary education curriculum can be rigid, with no flexibility in the teaching/learning process, assessment or content. In brief, secondary education in many countries is seen to be ill-prepared and ill-equipped to help students meet their current and future personal and social needs.

Other Recommendations for Development

Following are some further recommendations:

1. In any form of secondary education, students should be the key—all reform needs to be oriented towards students.
2. Reforming secondary education requires a holistic perspective in which all aspects should be involved. For example, critical and creative thinking skills for all students should be a central purpose of any educational reform, as should problem solving and national and international awareness. Furthermore, students should also be developing life, social and communication skills.
3. We need to look through the proposed models in more detail and choose the ones that suit the culture of each country. It is not necessary that one model fit all countries. Some of the models might not be suitable completely but some parts may be applicable.
4. There is a need to look beyond school-based management. It is good idea to give schools part of the responsibility of the school programme but there is a need to balance it with good system control and support.
5. The classroom environment in particular and school environment in general should develop the social skills of students alongside the intellectual or cognitive skills and capacities.
6. A more flexible environment is needed in schools and school systems to achieve the reform goals and produce better citizen.
7. The content of the school curriculum should be flexible and related to students' needs, lives and future careers. Furthermore, the concept or idea of "learning for life" also should be emphasized in reforming of secondary education.

8. There is a need to reform the teaching and learning processes as well as the assessment process to meet the goal of future secondary education.
9. It is important that the chance to be enrolled in secondary education is open to all who are in the age of this level.
10. Good collaboration is needed nationally and internationally in any reform. The reason is to share ideas and experiences with others. Therefore, governments, non-governmental organisations, community groups, private sector as well as the international organisation such as UNESCO and IBO should be participants in the reform process.
11. It is important that continuous assessment of any educational system is part of reform efforts.

Theme B: ***Effective New Models for Secondary Education in the 21st Century: The Focus for Change***

Dr. Muna bint Salim Al-Jardani

College of Education at Sultan Qaboos University

Number of Papers Presented: 18

Keynote Speaker	Professor J.S. Rajput, Director, National Council of Educational Research and Training, India
Topics	*Topic B.1:* World practices in dealing effectively with major dilemmas such as Balancing vocational and academic education, emphasizing knowledge and cognitive skills or behavioural and life skills, and designing systems for mass or selective education.

Topic B.2: Building better curriculum models.

Topic B.3: Best practices in assessment and strategic ways of changing methods of assessment.

Topic B.4: Application of educational technologies.

Topic B.5: Role of career guidance.

Topic B.6: Routes to cost effectiveness.

Introduction

In order for education to meet the needs of each society and its learners as well as the global arena, a huge reform agenda has been created. Papers presented in this theme draw attention to different types of tensions that exist within every education system worldwide. Some of these tensions arise between academic and vocational, global and local, tradition and modernity, individualism and community, homogeneity and heterogeneity, dependence and independence, and spiritual and practical.

The papers in this theme, which attempted to answer the question what are the areas of change, are organised into five major topics: balancing academic and vocational education, curriculum, integrating technology in education, assessment strategies, cost effectiveness, and career guidance.

1. Balancing Between the Dilemmas

Papers presented made the following recommendations:

- Integration between academic and vocational curricula (theoretical and practical aspects).
- Articulation and coherence between secondary and post-secondary education in terms of needs and skills.

- To balance quality and quantity of secondary education alternative strategies such as vocational, non-formal and distance education could be offered.
- Opening channels of communication between the different stakeholders and the Ministry of Education in developing and implementing any reforms in secondary education.
- Involvement of the private sector in planning and implementing secondary education reform (vocational and academic).
- Govermental and non-governmental organisations should collaborate in planning and implementing a comprehensive programme of academic and vocational education for secondary schools. These include Ministries, Councils of Development, private sector, regional (or willayates) representatives.
- To address the stigma associated with vocational education programmes we should:

  (i) raise people's awareness of the significant role of vocational education;

  (ii) build positive attitudes towards vocational education and instilling work values and ethics in youngsters.
- Assure equality in secondary education choices for all students including women and students with special needs.
- Concentration on generic transferable skills (all aspects of an industry) instead of skills that are hard to use in other work places.

2. Curriculum

Papers suggested the following:

- Secondary school curricula should acquaint learners with issues such as globalisation, information technology, life skills, sustainable development, education for peace, and the skills to live together.

- Expose students to a high level of cognitive (creative and critical thinking) and practical skills.
- Recognise the teacher's role in the reform of secondary education, especially in curriculum planning and design.
- Emphasising flexibility and diversity.
- Offering students a variety of choices according to their needs, interests and potentials.
- Stress the notion of self-learning and scientific research skills rather than just knowledge accumulation.
- Stress social cohesion and building a social person who is capable of living with other successfully.

3. *Integrating Technology into Education*

Papers offered the following recommendations:

- Information technology should be integrated in all subjects of the curriculum.
- Accommodating the cultural clash between the rapid pace of the advancement of technology and the slow change in the educational arena.

4. *Assessment*

The following recommendations were offered:

- Assessment systems need to have a suitable balance between reliability, validity, practicability, and compatibility with teaching in order to be effective.
- Should be based on assessing student problem solving and critical thinking.
- Should consist of both centrally and teacher produced examinations.

- Teachers should be provided with a clear framework for constructing tests so that they are comparable across schools.

5. Cost-effectiveness

Papers presented at this session suggested the following:

- Allocating sufficient funds for the new efforts in secondary education such as qualified teachers and up-to-date equipment.
- Participation in funding new secondary education by other contributors in the community (private sector and involved public institutions from other Ministries).
- Reducing the unit cost per student, teacher, class, school, textbook.
- Increasing internal efficiency, having better accountability and achieving economies of scale.
- Developing cost-sharing mechanisms such as tuition and user fees.

6. Career guidance

The two papers presented in this session suggested the following:

- Including career development and guidance for students starting from basic education through secondary education. For example, career exploration, work shadowing and other ways could be introduced.
- Students' needs and aspirations should be investigated and taken into account.
- Programme advice, guidance and counseling should reflect a comprehensive view of family, self-identity and career.
- Raising awareness of the importance of career guidance among students and their families.

Conclusion

I would like to emphasize an issue imbedded throughout the conference but not stressed well and in a straightforward way. It is the issue of maintaining the dignity of students, which I believe to be the ultimate goal of education. Many studies and personal observations showed that the curricula and the practices of school personnel, to some extent, marginalized student identity by ignoring their voices and choices. Twelve years of schooling has created a culture of silence and passive learners who are afraid to express themselves and who have a fear of public speech. In order to maintain students' dignity, students must be given the opportunity to express their authentic selves and discover their potentials. "Educate to be" is a major theme in this conference that is directly connected to preserving students' dignity. And I sincerely hope that it is not merely a slogan.

Theme C: Strategies for Successful Implementation of Reform: Practical Blueprints for Change

Dr. Ali bin Huwaishel Al-Shuely

College of Education at Sultan Qaboos University

Number of Papers Presented: 12

Keynote Speaker	Ms Carol Bates, Principal, Harris City Technology College, UK
Topics	*Topic C.1:* The role of the family and parents' involvement in strengthening community efforts to improve performance in secondary education.
	Topic C.2: Taking into account student needs.
	Topic C.3: Appropriate ways of involving the private and public sectors.

Topic C.4: Addressing labour market demands.

Topic C.5: Meeting the needs of post secondary education (academic and vocational).

Topic C.6: New trends in the preparation of teachers for the reform of secondary education: pre service and in service.

Topic C.7: The critical importance of leadership at all levels in managing educational change.

Topic C.8: Government approaches to policy and practice.

Introduction

"Education, not physical capital, has become the major source of present and future wealth of nations" (World Bank, 2000)

The qualitative and quantitative expansion of secondary education will result in necessity of proposing certain operational strategies for successful implementation of reform and suggest practical blueprints for change. In view of this issue, a keynote and other 12 speakers have highlighted a number of vital points and raised significant recommendations.

Such recommendations could be recombined and summed up as follows: the role of family and parents' involvement in improving performance in secondary education; taking into account student needs; ways of involving the private and public sectors and addressing labour market requirements; new trends in the preparation of teachers; and, the importance of leadership in managing educational change.

1. *Role of Family and Parents' Involvement in Improving Performance in Secondary Education*

- Due to globalisation and ongoing change, families should adopt a close cooperation between themselves and schools to maximize the benefits of home influence on students learning.
- Opportunity needs to be given for teachers to work collaboratively and efficiently with families and the broader school community and it is important to prepare teachers accordingly.
- It is preferable to make use of the media in order to help the community understand their role in developing secondary education.
- Families asked to be verbally rich with, and emotionally supportive of, their children.
- Adopt strategies and activities in order to encourage reluctant parents to re-establishing the link between the family and the school.
- Opening a forum for democratic decision-making including parents, student and other community members.
- Some schools experience difficulty when values conveyed at school many clash with those at home, thus dialogue between educators and parents aimed at developing a shared set of values which underpins all aspects of school life are essential.

Recommendations for teachers/parents counsels (TPC) include:

- ❒ Members of TPC should represent all parties comprising a community.
- ❒ The TPC board should be reconsidered and activated to include more parents and given more privileges.
- ❒ Scheduled and regular meetings should be held and attendance should be more welcomed.

- ❑ Members should be enthusiastically encouraged by different means, such as participating in school activities, media, and honouring them in formal educational gathering.

2. Taking into Account Student Needs

- There is a need to give assurance of support for collective efforts of all agencies and all social actors; family, school, media, community, youth organisation, as well as students.
- Diversify learning needs and interests, such as considering some continuing challenges including HIV/AIDS, drugs, violence, environment, education of girls, and child labour.
- Focus on promoting higher order skills and other mental abilities resulting in a more productive and creative learner.
- Expanding vocational/technical programmes in schools and, at the same time, updating crammed information.
- Giving opportunity to make secondary education available and accessible to all.
- For certain reasons and areas, distance and open education might be welcomed.
- Encourage cooperation and relationships among principals, deputies, teachers and students in order to develop a more healthy environment and release stress.

3. Ways of Involving the Private and Public Sectors and Addressing Labour Market Requirements

- Secondary education systems need to be redefined to align it with the current needs of the economy and society at large.
- Considering future needs of manpower and draw educational plans accordingly.

- All parties need to share information, pedagogy and experiences in order to improve the quality and relevance of the secondary education.
- Private (and public) sector institutions can play an important role in conducting some social investments and projects in
  - ❐ infrastructure,
  - ❐ supporting specific projects and certain schemes,
  - ❐ offering sponsorships; and
  - ❐ supporting curriculum in its components.
- Strengthen linkage of schools to the world of work through vocational guidance, study-work alternation and requirements of higher education and labour market.
- Give students opportunities to be involved in community service and apply their learning in work place and community, hosted by parents, family, community members, and local business and enterprises.

4. *New Trends in the Preparation of Teachers*

- Reform in teacher education must simultaneously accompany efforts toward school reform. There is a need to promote pre-secondary teachers in order to be able to teach in the secondary level through using effective strategies tailored for this specific purpose.
- Teacher preparation programmes need to consider abilities of individuals in light of their varying interests, aptitudes and stages of development and focus on the demands and need of the school.
- Ultimately, expert teachers could be the best judges of effective instructional strategies and should be given the latitude of working together to enhance the new system.

- Both teacher preparation institutions and schools must collaborate to prepare teachers in the way that they would be able to reform education and develop a future plan for teacher in-service.

- Programmes duration could be expanded to five years to give the required breadth and width.

- Criteria of candidate selection should be revised, especially for those prospective teachers intended to teach at the secondary level. In the terms of enrolment at colleges of education, new criteria are demanded to select the competent students to prepare them for this level of education. Percentage of GSCE should not be the only factor for gaining admission.

- Teaching practice period should be expanded to give student teachers more exposure to school life and activities.

- Consideration should be given to training centers with highly qualified personnel and enough facilities to meet the requirement of reform of education in all regions of the country.

- Teacher educators, especially those working in the in-service area, should be aware of the new trends in education.

- It is important to create a set of follow up strategies in acquainting teachers with the new trends in the education through longitudinal studies about their impact on their teaching.

5. Importance of Leadership in Managing Educational Change

- School principals should be equipped with knowledge and skills required to develop effective and continually improving schools.

- A typological framework for a comparative analysis of international models of leadership development should be outlined.

- Consideration should be given to adopting school autonomy and decentralisation in the management of secondary education.
- There is a need to set up criteria for selection for administrative roles.
- Emphasise the concept of efficient school administration that utilizes modern administrative technique and human and other resources available.
- Adopt an effective instructional matrix as an instructional strategy and train teachers in its use. Utilizing the experiences of countries using the instructional matrix.
- There is a need to keep up the qualfications of educational leaders in order that they can function professionally in their specific contexts.
- We need to distinguish between leadership as a function (which all can do) and leadership as a role (which might be held by the qualified position holder, such as the principal).
- Develop a strategy to have all stakeholders (including students) involved, including offering students some responsibility.
- It is very preferable that a rotation policy be conducted through which a principal running a particular school would after an agreed duration would move to another school in order to maximize managerial experiences among several in each school and among communities of schools.

Theme D: Practices in Evaluating the Success of Reform

Dr. Salma bint Hamad Al-Humaidi

College of Education at Sultan Qaboos University

Number of Papers Presented: 10

Keynote Speaker Professor James Popham, UCLA

Topics

Topic D.1: Accountability: setting and meeting standards.

Topic D.2: Maximising access, opportunity and completion rates.

Topic D.3: Measuring improvement in educational outcomes.

Topic D.4: Examining indicators of capacity building at the school and community level.

Introduction

"The provision of an education of quality for all requires a holistic approach to teaching and learning, and to the development of the human kind in general. The environmental conditions and contexts at home, in the community, at school and in the classroom have direct bearings on the quality of teaching, and on learning achievement in particular. The later is often measured through high-stakes examinations, which in turn, are used to screen out, to select and push out the majority from the elected few, for future educational or occupational opportunities." (Keynote paper by Chinapah, 2002)

The theme of evaluation resulted in different sub-themes: accountability; participatory planning and decentralisation; maximizing access, opportunity and completion rates; and, quality education for all. *Following are the main recommendations for each sub-theme.*

1. Accountability

- There is a need to undertake more research on accountability and in so doing focus on its applicability for different organisations, especially service organisations.

- Research on improving schools needs to bear the current press from accountability in mind.
- Schools must be evaluated differently according to the stage of development they have reached.
- In education we should have smarter ways of evaluation related to accountability, which suits our society and education system.
- Schools need to self-evaluate and model what is suitable for itself.
- School reform evaluation should be summative in nature but that evaluation should be focused on educationai improvement rather than on dispassionate appraisal.
- Instructionally supportive assessments should be used to evaluate students. These assessments, or tests, should possess four characteristics—importance, describability, reportability, and reachability.

2. ***Participatory Planning and Decentralisation***

- Participatory policy planning should depend on a clear philosophical basis.
- Collaborative planning is important to school improvement. It is a process that takes time to be fruitful. However, it is worth the effort, especially when we realise its beneficial effects on learning and teaching. *The benefits include:*
  - ❒ working together as a team;
  - ❒ supporting each other;
  - ❒ mutual understanding between students and teachers; and
  - ❒ student achievement is improved.
- Creation of regional and sub-regional networks, such as in the Gulf States, should provide the

basis for a more useful continuing dialogue on reforms across the world.

- Adopt the concept of partnership and prepare all those to be involved to take decisions. Benefits should be obtained from partnerships between schools and other parties otherwise these partnerships might die.
- If we are to move effectively towards decentralisation of an educational system, we need to have adequate mutual understanding of roles and responsibilities.
- Cooperation of governmental and non-governmental organisations would enrich the educational experiences of schools and the methods of developing innovations in the whole education system.
- Deal with the current mentality by raising awareness and realisations of individuals in education about their importance.

3. *Maximizing Access, Opportunity and Completion Rates*

In 1997 in England the government announced a policy which stated: "While recognising the paramount importance of meeting the needs of individual children, and the necessity of the specialist provision for some, we shall promote the inclusion of children within mainstream schooling wherever possible." (paper by Pearson, 2002) This policy was referring specifically to pupils with special educational needs. Other governments have taken a broader view of inclusion including any group, which might be marginalized, such as ethnic minorities and gifted and talented.

- A need for introducing inclusion in its many aspects as social and developmental cohesion, including integrating students who suffer serious difficulties.
- A need for a change in schools in order to develop inclusion in respect of organisation, culture and practices.

- Need to provide training for teachers and sufficient materials and equipment.
- Allow enough time for making change.
- Allow for exchange of experiences among countries.

4. ***Quality Education for All***

- More attention should be given to curriculum planning in a way that makes it more learner centred and relevant to students' daily lives.
- Special consideration should be given teacher education programmes.
- Systematic and continuous assessment is needed in order to better understand the dynamics of the teaching and learning context.
- The home environment plays an important role in pupils' learning achievement.
- Parents need to be encouraged to play an active role in promoting quality education
- The goals of secondary education should take social and economic needs and globalisation pressures into consideration.
- There is a need to involve principals in, and provide counseling sessions for, teacher's inspection.
- OECD's Programme for International Student Assessment (PISA) needs to be given greater attention. PISA is a longitudinal study with assessment of Maths, Science and Reading literacy skills of 15-year-old students in at least 32 countries every three years. "The strength of PISA is not to rank countries on one list summarizing their total educational outputs in one number only. The wealth of information that was collected is reported in such a way that it places emphasis on

profiles of countries giving educational authorities the tools to compare the profile of their country with their policies and those of other countries, and to monitor changes to a country's profile over time." (Paper by Bakker, 2002)

So referring to PISA, the following recommendations were made:

- ❒ countries can benefit from PISA;
- ❒ do not use the test to make comparison between countries;
- adapt such projects to local situations including developing instruments to measure learning improvement at the national and sub-regional levels;
- preparation for acceptance of test results needs to be part of the process;
- understand and highlight the context of specific countries for more meaningful interpretation of results;
- there is a need to continue to collect more information about the student, such as his or her home educational environment or socio-economic status; and,
- there is a need to support the idea of having tools other than exams for evaluating students.

Theme E: Sharing New Ideas

Dr. Salha Abdullah Issan

College of Education at Sultan Qaboos University

Number of Papers Presented: 16

Keynote Speaker	HE Dr Ali Fakhro, Kingdom of Bahrain
Topics	*Topic E.1:* Sharing ideas from different countries

Topic E.2: Sharing ideas on labour market and manpower issues

Topic E.3: Sharing ideas on curriculum

Introduction

As economic, social and technological changes gathers pace, people everywhere need to develop their knowledge and skills, on a continuing basis, so that they can live and work meaningfully in the knowledge society. It follows that education and training at the secondary level can also help individuals to participate in economic growth and social development. The effort to develop secondary education for all school leavers is to ensure their opportunities to acquire new skills and knowledge that will help them to pursue higher education, and/or to give them a chance in life and work.

Models and experimentations presented in the conference by different speakers reflect acknowledged policies and practices. The papers seek to guide national-decision-makers to develop effective, relevant and equitable policies of education and training for secondary level. They also seek to engage other stakeholders—including the social partners, to support their policies and practices.

The papers also:

- reflected on the new realities facing societies under study (changing role of secondary education, globalisation and educational challenges, need for constant renewal of knowledge, need for professional development, changing educational stereotype, privatisation, social inequalities, a value orientation and engagement of stakeholders);
- responding to the challenges through curricula development, institutional reorganisation, better learning and teaching materials and equipment,

improvement in school management, and restructuring of initial teacher education and professional development;

- show that evaluation and assessment has been seen as formative rather than summative. It is directed to validate the whole educational organisation rather than the student's achievement and progress. Accountability of those concerned is linked to systematic assessment and the educational institution is evaluated by the whole society to be sure of its efficiency and effectiveness; and,
- many recommendations and recommendations mentioned in reports have already included in the previous themes.

Sharing Ideas from Different Countries

Sixteen papers addressing this theme described different projects and modalities of developing secondary education in term of facilities, machinery, equipment, curriculum contents, development of software and other instructional materials. Students and teachers are offered opportunities to participate in these projects and research carried on in some of these countries. Most of these countries have either formed effective organisation of secondary education or are moving in that direction. Never the less it is obvious that in many countries significant gaps still exist between secondary education and society's and students' needs.

1. India

"The Re-defining Secondary Education for 21st Century" offers some successful examples of co-operative training between industry and secondary schools, encouraging women and girls to join vocational training, offering parallel, flexible, non formal schooling for those who are unable to join formal schools. Attention has been directed to encourage females in secondary schools to join vocational streams to make balance in manpower recruitment at different sectors of economy. The experiences of the central board of secondary education in humanizing the curricular institutional and system responses to address both the conceptual and operational segments of change dynamics are presented in the paper with relevant examples and care studies.

2. *Bahrain*

"The new effective models to reform secondary education in the Kingdom of Bahrain". The paper highlights the model of local networks of communications in secondary schools. It refers to the mechanism of using computer laboratories in a diversified secondary school. It refers to promoting introduction of the Internet in implementing students' projects that serve school students at facilitate communication with other schools. It gives details about the practical model of the commercial and technical education. It highlights the procedures of providing professional guidance and orientation for schools leavers. It also gives details about the GLOBE project, which has been implemented in secondary school in collaboration with the U.S.A. Embassy in Bahrain to facilitate learning sciences.

3. *Uganda*

"Maximizing access, opportunity, completion rates regarding Secondary Education": This paper explains the policy reforms Uganda is trying to undertake to maximize access and opportunities for students at secondary schools. Different board policy options are selected from a menu of possible strategies for meeting the challenges facing secondary education. The paper also refers to the issue of maximizing school effectiveness with a limited budget.

4. *Japan*

"Major challenges and dilemma that faces secondary education now and in future, and the role of reforms in meeting these challenges and dilemma". This paper presented data collected from an investigation on Japanese secondary education and its curriculum over a period of five years by using sociological methods. It reveals that discussion on reform of curriculum should be based on the data collected from schools. The reformers planned these curricula from their own perspective for the 21st century without involving the practitioners at schools. The optional courses and cross-curriculum activities being established require various changes to meet the future needs.

5. Oman

"Teaching strategies for Secondary Education". This paper proposed methods, which can enhance students' understanding, develop abilities to work with others, and attend to thinking skills and aptitudes. These methods are: cooperative learning, problem solving, discovery-inquiry, concept mapping, the project and case study methods. The researcher highlighted that increase flexibility of study programmes demand changing teaching strategies for secondary education.

"Challenge facing Technical Education in The Royal Air Force of Oman". The general purpose of this paper is to shed some light on the challenges facing technical training in The Royal Air Force of Oman (RAFO). It put forward recommendations for bridging the gaps between general education and further education. IT highlights the skills shortages for all the students applied for RAFO, which is considered the biggest challenge facing technical training. The new entrants lack competencies in various areas such as Basic English, Maths and vocational skills. To achieve the integration between schools and work, ideological cultural barriers between education and enterprises must be broke down. Technical subject areas that are in high demand should be considered, while maintaining some of the traditional subject.

"A proposed formula for development of Secondary Education in the light of trends of vocational schools in the Sultanate of Oman". The paper is concerned with development of vocational Secondary Education for girls. Statistics of 2001 shows that despite the cost 55.9% of Secondary Schools leavers are not qualified to join labour market. The objective of the study is to identify the interests of Omani girls with regard to vocational education. A random sample of 329 female students at grade 11-12, graduates of secondary schools, parents and employers were selected. Four different questionnaires were designed. The data analysis reveals the following: 92% of the girls like to join vocational education, 93% of parents would like that their daughters join vocational education programmes so they can easily be employed, 74% of the employers believe that efficiency and experience are the most important factor in hiring secondary graduates (whether males or females).

6. Malaysia

"Towards building a better curriculum models for Science Education in Malaysian secondary schools: A scientist entrepreneurial approach". This study highlights that Malaysian secondary school students' performance in sciences is declining due to several factors. It proposed a new science curriculum model, which integrates science process, skills and entrepreneurial thinking as a way to attract secondary students, interest and motivation to learn sciences.

7. Egypt

"A Proposed Model for the content of the mathematics curriculum in Secondary Education in the light of the current professional requirements". The paper reviews models for the content of mathematics in technical education in the light of contemporary professional requirements. The paper directs attention to the issue of identifying the mathematics content requirement for student in different vocational branches in Egyptian secondary schools (agricultural, commercial, and industrial). Mathematical modeling is also important in introducing mathematics that is relevant to actual life. The paper suggests a model suitable for organizing mathematics content in technical education in Egypt.

8. Sudan

"The current status of the Secondary Education: Special focus in Sudan" The paper gives general view of the Sudanese Secondary Education system, its foundations, aims, and quality of its outcomes. It refers to the requirements of the sustainable comprehensive development. It argues that the Improvement projects should meet the values, traditions, culture and heritage of the Sudanese society and qualify citizens to be capable of interacting in the world of tomorrow. It emphasizes the supportive role of the private sector in enforcing better Secondary Education.

9. Palestine

"Current status of secondary Education in Palestine and its Development for better future". The paper described the Palestinian Education system, its curricula and programmes. It reflected on the innovation implemented in 11-12 grades based on offering two main streams (academic and technical). The Education and Training Council for Vocational and Technical Education supervises the technical stream. The paper highlights the constraints and pressures the secondary school students face every day as a result of Israelis' occupation. The government has taken special measures to ensure higher male and female student completion to in both academic and technical training.

10. Qatar

"Reform of the educational system in Qatar—The scientific school model" This paper focuses on the scientific School Model which was initiated in the academic year 1999/2000. The project is considered as a starting point to a comprehensive educational development in Qatar. This model is adopted from the American scientific school with some changes to cope with the Qatari society. The project is under assessment and continuous evaluation to validate its effectiveness.

Sharing Ideas about Curriculum

1. Futurizing

"Futurizing the transaction of curriculum". This paper aims at highlighting the importance of curriculum and how to improve education through improving curriculum. It refers to the importance of creative activities. Project methods can be considered as priorities in acquisition of knowledge, work experience, and society's understanding. Many professionals and stakeholders should participate in determining the curriculum content for future.

2. Problem-based Learning

"Implementing problem based learning in the science and mathematics classroom: A Method of involving minority and female students". This paper aims at examining the effectiveness of problem: based learning on students' understanding in the middle grades in maths and science classroom. Data identified the components of changes in students' learning processes. These components included self-confidence, group dynamics, self-motivation and independence. This method can be successful to help students at risk of failing. Overall, this study suggested strong potential for problem based learning as a useful tool for learning through life.

3. Science

"The status of science education in the secondary school, its challenges and the role of epistemology and meta-cognition in its reforms". The paper highlights the problems of teaching practice for the prospective teachers in secondary schools at national and international level. These problems are related to science teachers, their supervisor and cooperative teachers and their limited understanding of scientific concepts and their application in real life. The researcher refers to some trends, which may contribute to improvements in teaching sciences. He states that reform in teaching practice and science teaching/ learning may be accomplished through addressing the epistemology and meta-cognition.

4. Closer Links Between Schools and the Economic Sector

"To what extend is national education systems considered as the main gate to economic competition?" The paper highlights the national educational suggestion in some selected countries (UK, America and Japan) in the promotion of closer linkage between schools and the economic sectors. Recent technological developments have made increased demands for mobility and skill diversification on the work force. The paper concludes with evaluation of Omani current policy issues in an attempt to specify the extent to which it is suitable for the government to interfere in Vocational Education. Most of the case studies revealed that the education and its content are considered as an essential factor to determine economic growth and progress.

Summary and Recommendations

The papers in Theme *E* can be summarized as follows:

- In almost all reporting countries, secondary education is seen as a means of human resources development, leading to social and economic progress.
- Some of the papers underline the rate at which secondary education will need to grow to keep pace with new influx of knowledge and technological developments and providing learners with skills required in the changing structure of the economy.
- Budgetary constraints have limited the full development of secondary education.
- Recognition of the need to introduce various forms of academic and vocational guidance services to help secondary school leavers to cope with the word outside school.
- Studies and reports presented refer to the introduction of new technologies, such as computers,

Internet, television, ICT, etc, in curricula to enable students to keep pace with scientific and technological advances. As such technologies are costly, generous contribution of hardware and software by various agencies is required.

- Most studies emphasize the importance of teacher initial education and training and describe various measures to be taken to improve the quality of teacher's education.
- Exchanges of information and experiences and training activities through institutional linkage are suggested.
- UNESCO has an important role in initiating innovation programmes to help member states in their efforts to develop secondary education.
- Research on secondary education is essential and should be carried out on a large scale—at national and international levels.

Recommendations for reform of secondary education can be summarized as follows:

- Secondary education should be assigned the role and function of inducting the learners (males and females) into higher educational institutions and life itself.
- Information, experiences and findings from implementing new projects or models should be studied and analyzed and circulated among member states of UNESCO. This procedure would allow more dialogue and diagnosis of their effectiveness.
- The expansion of innovations and projects related to secondary education development should be based on systematic evaluation and assessment.
- To achieve integration with the society, schools should open their doors for professionals from

industry, commerce and services to participate in teaching certain courses or programmes related to their specialisations.

- Secondary school curricular should be flexible to allow more freedom without neglecting the core curriculum, which is essential to ensure cohesion among learners.
- There is a need for qualified teaching staff possessing adequate academic and pedagogical qualification, coupled with practical experiences, including being trained to apply new strategies of teaching and learning.
- Countries should set up criteria to control the quality of teaching by using accountability, accreditation and professionalism principles.
- Staff qualification, and reasonable ratios of teaching and training staff to learners is demanded if secondary education aims to achieve the integration of academic and technical programmes with secondary schools.
- In order to help female students adapt to the requirements of new technologies and labour market demands, they should be offered vocational and technical education, which is equal to that offered for male students.
- Introduction of information technology requires competent technicians. Therefore, it is essential to direct more attention to this group in order to fully perform their duties at schools.
- Schools need to be provided with equipments and materials, which enrich application, particularly in sciences, maths and technical subjects.
- Secondary school management should be based on collaborative principles and staff involvement in planning and implementation of schools programme and activities.

Conclusion

To conclude, international educational agencies, researchers, policy makers, and practitioners have been offered advice on how curricular at secondary school can be linked to practical concerns but it is clear that local planners are also essential because they are more aware of their society's conditions. As secondary education can be expensive, the dilemma is how to provide quality secondary education and solve the problem of cost.

II. Recommendations from Other Recent UNESCO Reports on Secondary Education

The recommendations from other recent reports are summarised in what follows. They are based on:

- UNESCO. (2001) Executive summary: Meeting agreements. *International expert meeting on general Secondary Education in the Twenty-first Century: Trends, challenges and priorities.* Paris: UNESCO Final Report on the meeting held in Beijing, People's Republic of China, May 21-25.
- Billeh, V., BouJaoude, S., & Sulieman, S. (2002). *Regional synthesis on development of Secondary Education in the Arab States.* Beirut: UNESCO Regional Office, December.
- Zhou Nan-zhao & Haw, G. (2002). *Secondary education reforms in Asia-Pacific region: Challenges, strategies and programme actions in addressing learners' needs.* A report on the 8th UNESCO-APEID International Conference in Education held in Bangkok 26-29 November, 2002 and presented as a paper at Sultanate of Oman Ministry of Education/UNESCO International Conference Secondary Education for a Better Future: Trends, Challenges and Priorities, Muscat, Sultanate of Oman, 22-24 December.
- UNESCO Dakar Regional Office. (2002). *General report of the regional workshop on the reform of*

Secondary Education in Africa. Mauritius, 3-6 December.

- Oman/Ministry of Education. (2002). *Recommendations of the national seminar on Secondary Education.* Muscat, 1-3 April.

UNESCO. (2001) Executive Summary: Meeting Agreements. *International Expert Meeting on General Secondary Education in the Twenty-first Century: Trends, Challenges and Priorities.* Paris: UNESCO Final Report on the Meeting Held in Beijing, People's Republic of China, May 21-25.

1. **Secondary Education (SE) should be given high priority.**
2. **The objectives and functions of SE need to be redefined for the twenty-first century and in a way that effectively addresses the themes, or dilemmas, facing it, such as mass and selective schooling, general and selective (vocational) education, and cognitive and behavioural outcomes.**
3. ***In Respect of Mass and Selective Schooling***
   1. Countries should continue to be committed to the goal of mass SE as a minimum in terms of policy and provision.
   2. Commitment to universal access to SE as an aspiration should be maintained with efforts to remove barriers and obstacles as well as build on strengths and opportunities.
   3. Serious attention be given to making adequate provision for those not selected into SE, those who drop out or leave before completing the cycle and those denied access to their preferred streams.
   4. Where there is not full transition from Primary to Secondary and/or from lower Secondary to upper Secondary, efforts must be made to accommodate

all those who are eligible through alternative provisions. Where this is not possible available places should be allocated equitably and transparently.

5. Mass access to SE will require partnership between governments and other providers (private, NGOs, etc.), but governments should seek to safeguard the interests of learners by ensuring standards are maintained by all providers.
6. The structure of programmes and streaming practices should be reviewed to offer greater flexibility and choice to learners in the selection process, including the option to return to a preferred stream.
7. Future orientation at Secondary should be towards greater diversity of what is provided, more flexibility in the organisation of learning and greater responsiveness to the needs and circumstances of learners.

4. *In respect of General and Selective (Vocational) Education*

1. The SE system should focus on links between academic and vocational subjects and their interdependence in the overall education of adolescent learners.
2. SE is about preparation for life and should reflect the reality of life in the twenty-first century that encompasses a seamless to-and-fro between continued learning and the world of work.
3. The nature of Vocational subjects, the way in which they are organised and taught, as well as the recognition given to them determine their status in the Secondary school curriculum.
4. SE, including Vocational Education (VE), needs to address not only the human resource needs of the

society but also the development needs and aspirations of the individual.

5. There is a strong trend in SE in most countries to include some element of VE for all learners. Some countries are experimenting with ways of providing such joint education to different population groups, including migrants, isolated rural populations and learners in regular Secondary schools.
6. Incorporating VE into SE can be expensive resulting in poor teaching and a lowering of status of these subjects. Innovative and cost-effective strategies to overcome this problem have included contracting out the teaching of subjects to nearby specialist schools and centres or creating different ways of teaching Vocational disciplines that are less demanding in terms of equipment, materials and practically trained instructors.
7. As the trend of lifelong learning is becoming clear, SE is adjusting to this reality by developing flexible structures and varied options in their programmes, as well as having stronger links to the world of work.

5. In respect of Cognitive and Behavioural Outcomes

1. There is recognition that traditional academically based education does not adequately address students' needs in terms of realizing their full potential, especially in a context of rapid economic, cultural and social change.
2. Given the declining role of other socializing agencies schools should take greater responsibility for helping learners acquire life-skills.
3. The emerging role of teachers (notably as facilitators), their status, integrity and commitment are essential for implementing life skills education successfully. The quality of pre-service and in-Service teacher training is critical in this regard.

4. Teaching methods, school facilities and services should be developed and adapted to provide life-skills/behavioural education.

5. The role of Secondary school principals needs to be consistent with this new reality.

6. Education decision-makers need to be sensitised to the consequences of their choices based on evidence of such factors as the links between academic success and personal and community well being.

7. A multi-sectoral approach involving government ministries, NGOs local communities, etc. is essential for successful implementation of this kind of education.

6. *Other Identified Themes that SE is, or will be, Facing in Achieving its New Objectives and Functions Included:*

1. Inclusive and compensatory education.
2. Holistic and participatory education.
3. Strengthening equity.
4. The effective use of information communications technology.

7. *Resources and/or Strategies Needed to Respond to the New Objectives and Functions of SE and to Manage the Themes or Dilemmas Include:*

1. Commencing with the view that students are at the centre of any education reform.

2. Understanding that there are three interrelated components to support students' learning—the people, whether educational professionals, parents or community members, the educational policies that offer a framework for what students need to learn, and the infrastructure.

8. UNESCO's Assistance is Sought to Help Attain the Following in Relation to These Three Interrelated Components:

1. For students
   - *(i)* Reconstructing SE to ensure a consideration of learners' diversified needs and provide them with knowledge and life-long skills including vocational learning.
2. For teachers, curriculum and school
   - *(i)* Giving priority to teacher education (pre-service and in-service).
   - *(ii)* Ensuring that the curricula present goals and objectives clearly and precisely and reflect local needs—including socio-economic needs.
   - *(iii)* Ensuring schools both understand and have the ability to become learning organisations/learning communities.
3. For infrastructure and policy
   - *(i)* Ensuring that policy-makers stress and give enough attention to SE.
   - *(ii)* Providing access to SE by providing a place for all learners.
   - *(iii)* Offering appropriate resources for SE through adequate budget allocations.

9. Recommendations for Future UNESCO Activities:

1. Providing written case studies and/or a data base of successful practice in SE with a focus on
   - *(i)* Vocational Education
   - *(ii)* distance learning and information communications technology
   - *(iii)* life-skills and life-long education
   - *(iv)* discovery learning
   - *(v)* the changing role of teachers and the use of roles other than teachers in schools

- *(vi)* pre-service and in-service teacher education and increasing the status of teachers
- *(vii)* assessment literacy (i.e., having and being able to use assessment with predictive validity) and evidence-informed policy and accountability
- *(viii)* capacity building or organisational learning/ learning community
- *(ix)* whole-of-government approaches to policy and practice
- *(x)* the balance between administrative and curriculum centralisation and decentralisation
- *(xi)* complementary and alternative provision of resources.

2. Organise forums and facilitating international exchange and cooperation in the area of SE leading to a major World Education Forum on Secondary Education.
3. Continue to provide a vehicle for establishing the ideals and for holding governments accountable for moving towards these ideals.

Billeh, V., BouJaoude, S., & Sulieman, S. (2002). *Regional Synthesis on Development of Secondary Education in the Arab States*. Beirut: UNESCO Regional Office, December.

Recommendations

1. There is a need for secondary education to be flexible and responsive to the needs of learners in the twenty first century. This requires that we design curricula that will allow students to keep abreast of changes taking place in all fields of knowledge. Thus emphasis should be on providing students with knowledge, but more importantly with skills for lifelong learning.
2. There needs to be a movement from centralised to decentralised styles of school and educational

system management. International trends point out the importance of school-based management and moving the decision making process closest to the school and students. This will require a more participatory approach to management at all educational levels. These changes may help in improving the efficiency and effectiveness of the educational system.

3. There is a need for more networking among countries and regions regarding secondary education reform. Many countries have attempted to reform their secondary education and lessons can be learned from the successes and failures of these countries.

4. Secondary education goals have to be linked more to sustainable development, citizenship, and the world of work. However, while school to work approaches to education are very important, this should be done without sacrificing knowledge for its own sake.

5. The traditional concepts of educational personnel training seem to emphasise their passive role in the process. However, contemporary international trends recommend more active roles for teachers and other educational personnel in their professional development.

6. There needs to be more emphases on quality technical and vocational education and training. This branch of secondary education should be relegated to those students who cannot join the general education (academic) streams.

7. Students in secondary schools should be encouraged to be active in the teaching-learning process. This is important in all subject areas, especially when students are introduced to information and communication technology (ICTs). If students continue playing a passive role in their

learning, they will always be on the receiving and will never become active and creative producers of knowledge.

Zhou Nan-zhao & Haw, G. (2002). *Secondary Education Reforms in Asia-Pacific Region: Challenges, Strategies and Programme Actions in Addressing Learners' Needs.* A report on the 8th UNESCO-APEID International Conference in Education Held in Bangkok 26-29 November, 2002 and presented as a paper at Sultanate of Oman Ministry of Education/UNESCO International Conference Secondary Education for a Better Future: Trends, Challenges and Priorities, Muscat, Sultanate of Oman, 22-24 December.

Conference Outcomes and Recommendations

In the final session of the conference, the major recommendations from all activities conducted over the period of the conference were aggregated into a comprehensive set of recommendations that was adopted by delegates at the conference.

1. It is essential that educators and policy makers must take active steps to address the multifaceted needs of adolescents. These include educational strategies, but also extend to other areas such as psychological, health and social actions.
2. In order to meet the varied needs of adolescents, it remains most crucial to enlist the collective efforts of all agencies and all social actors. Political commitment has to be made by governments, schools, media, and civic societies to assure the rights of adolescents to basic education, health and other necessary services in light of Dakar Framework of Action. Such strategies must include:

   1. Multi-sectoral cooperation [education, health, labor, environment, youth, women, social welfare, public security, etc] in policies, planning, favourable environment and resources mobilisation... [and

including] formal education agencies like school, non-formal education agencies like worksites, radio, TV and informal agencies like homes, libraries, market.

2. Participatory approaches: involvement of the grass roots—family, school, the media, communities, as well as adolescents themselves, youth organisations.
3. Inter-agency coordination, with appropriate division of work to avoid duplication and waste of resources.
4. Inter-disciplinary and integrated programme/activities for holistic development to address adolescents' needs in holistic ways.
5. Partnership and networking for efficiency and effectiveness of programme implementation.

3. To address the varied adolescents' needs, intersectoral and interagency cooperation and coordination remains crucial for success in programme design and implementation. Among possible areas of cooperation for consideration could be the following:
   1. Policy guidelines developed for holistic systemic secondary education reform.
   2. Secondary education for out-of-school youth, through alternative programmes.
   3. Curricular innovations and teacher training for learning universally shared values for upgraded moral/ethical standards.
   4. Development of core indicators of quality of secondary education: assessment of multi-dimensional learning achievements.
   5. School health both physical and psychological (e.g. flagship FRESH Programme, psychological counseling at school; culturally appropriate, broad-

based adolescents reproductive health, preventive education against HIV/AIDS).

6. Vocational guidance for school-to work linkage and transition.

7. Creative use of ICT in help meet adolescents needs: not only 'growing digital' but maturing affectively, not only 'high tech' but 'high touch'.

8. Listening to the voices of adolescents and fostering cooperation among youth: supporting World Scouts, Asia-Pacific Youth Forum, and Youth Camps in promoting international understanding and inter-cultural learning; youth seminars, films, sports and physical education, etc.

9. Youth capacity building: youth leaders training programmes.

10. Partnership and networking with youth associations like the World Scout Organisation, NGOs, ASPnet, UNESCO Clubs, and national/ local authorities (e.g. ASP schools and IBO schools as pioneers in building four pillars of quality education).

4. Policy dialogue on key issues and encourage the development of policy guidelines for holistic systemic structural reforms, such as:

1. expansion through formal, non-formal, informal and ICT-assisted open learning systems;

2. diversification through general and vocational education;

3. gender equity;

4. favourable learning environments;

5. recognition of different learning experiences by labour market; and,

6. public-private partnerships.

5. Provide proactive technical assistance to member countries for the improvement of quality or secondary education, using:
   1. learner-centred curricular reforms;
   2. training and professional development for teachers and principals; and,
   3. assessment of multiple dimensions of learning achievements in terms of knowledge, skills, competencies and values/changes attitudes and behaviours.
6. Assist in national capacity-building through joint materials development and training of trainers programmes for:
   1. policy-makers at central and local levels for decentralisation;
   2. school headmasters for school-based management;
   3. teachers for continued professional development; and,
   4. curriculum specialists.
7. Promote:
   1. diverse modes of learning for in- and out-of-school youth;
   2. linkages of school to the world of work, with increased stress on alternation of study and work, and vocational guidance for school-work transition; and,
   3. public-private partnerships and regional networking, for the mobilisation of resources employment of school leavers.

The APEID Conference also finally endorsed the recommendation of the 1998 Melbourne UNESCO Conference on Secondary Education, which stated in part:

The Conference recommends a major review of secondary education involving a similarly broad group of participants as at Jomtien.... The bridging role of secondary education has never been more difficult or more important. The enormous expansion of this sector from a selective pattern for a few, to one of increasingly universal participation, has brought with it a confusion of purpose and an uncertainty about role, which has made secondary education the subject of criticism as well as concern. The education and work interface is most sensitive here. The turbulence of adolescence has most impact here. The competition for entry to higher education is most keenly felt here. As the Delors Report said, 'Many of the hopes and criticisms aroused by formal systems seem to focus on secondary education.' This is a global priority.

The Conference also endorsed the following statement from Melbourne:

> ... it is recommended that UNESCO continue and increase its endeavours in promoting the value of secondary education for all, and that Governments and educational policy-makers give high priority in planning and allocation of resources to ensure that this is achieved.

UNESCO Dakar Regional Office. (2002). *General Report of the Regional Workshop on the Reform of Secondary Education in Africa. Mauritius, 3-6 December.*

Conclusions and Recommendations of the Workshop

Theme 1: Involving Stakeholders, Parents, Students and Other Communities in the Management and Governance of Secondary Education:

4. General conclusions and recommendations:

   1. There is need to involve religious groups and other stakeholders in education.
   2. There is need to involve actively the parents, teachers and students in the school governance in order to realise the highest degree of ownership at school level.
   3. Governments should provide appropriate structures and resources to support educational

institutions and should not centralise their management, as this is likely to stifle institutional creativity and progress.

4. In order to reduce geographic disparities within and across districts/provinces, the governments should provide basic infrastructure, resources and incentives to the educational institutions.

5. Creation of local community secondary schools leads to increased transition rates from primary to secondary school and decreased number of boarding schools, which would be more cost effective.

6. Creation of enabling environment should include among others: Leadership within the community; Commitment to change at local level; Clearly stated system of representatives; and, Transparency.

7. Secondary Education should provide school leavers who are functionally ready for world of work as well as being ready for tertiary education.

8. There should be a move to decentralisation of management of the school systems so that there is some flexibility for regional and local level school administration to adjust the curriculum to local needs, recruit the type of staff needed and even involve parents and other stakeholders in educational decision that support them.

9. Consideration of a child as a human social asset should warrant active involvement of all relevant stakeholders.

10. There is need for tailor-made training to all various stakeholders at different levels of involvement and participation.

11. Involve grassroots communities in the financing, management and governance of secondary education.

12. Provide support for private initiatives in secondary education.

13. Initiate learning to live together by laying more emphasis on moral and human values and especially values of tolerance, dialogue and mutual listening in secondary education.
14. Initiate the establishment of human rights clubs within the framework of pre-school activities.
15. Promote self-empowerment students.
16. Provide financial support for grassroots communities in their efforts made in secondary Education.
17. Enhance co-operation in secondary education especially in terms of infrastructure, education materials, textbooks and training streams diversification.
18. Provide real support for capacity development at the level of in-service training as well as at the institutional and logistic levels.
19. Provide special support for countries in crisis or going out of crisis and thus promote reintegration in education or in working life.
20. Support private initiatives in secondary education.
21. Pursue reflection on the renovation of secondary education by organising meetings of this type.
22. Follow up these workshop recommendations.
23. Provide technical co-operation in the formulation of secondary education reforms for countries that need it
24. Provide technical support in educational policies to be implemented within the framework of foreign debt cancellation or reduction.

Theme II: Development of Curriculum and Assessment

5. General conclusions and recommendations

1. Societies need some social stability and economic stability. Education is not sufficient, on its own, to

guarantee this, but it is an essential prerequisite to social stability or economic development. In an interdependent world, social instability or economic deprivation in any state or region has repercussions around the world imperative.

2. In this respect, secondary education is crucial because, it is during adolescence that most social tensions are formed and during which most foundation skills of the development of "economic-activity potential" are formed.

3. Curiosity, creativity and energy are "natural" components of the human condition. The question poses a challenge to education systems to provide learning experiences, which maintain (through adolescence) these natural human attributes. It should be taken as an accepted fact that all adolescents have high motivation, in wait for training.

4. Education systems have traditionally directed and selected students. Many systems continue to be engaged in the process of closing doors rather than opening doors. It is an imperative that secondary education be general and inclusive, such that paths of future learning and training are kept open to all students.

   This implies Literacy, numeracy and technological literacy are identified as key "life-skills" and are promoted as such. An emphasis on "learning to do" such that the student is able to take on challenges with confidence and at any time. "Learning to do" may be seen as "skills in the application of knowledge" (as opposed to knowledge-acquisition alone).

5. A proper linkage between vocational and general secondary education is easing the difficulties of

transition between school and work. It can be developed by vocationalising general education, which is skills should be taught parallel to normal academic education. So that, every secondary school learner possesses those skills.

6. Core curriculum and teaching methods for youth on issues such as inter-ethnic respect, conflict resolution and mediation that build the right behaviours and attitudes in young people are developed by including life skills in curriculum and using problem solving teaching methods. Students should also be exposed to those problems and lefts to work for solutions on their own.

7. Secondary Education Curricula should be developed based on study or research of the real economic and socio-cultural needs of the given country. It should also take into consideration the modern trends in internationalisation and globalisation.

8. Teachers play a central role to improve the quality of education and deliver the new curriculum. Teachers who lack the knowledge and skills of different subjects and there are not capable of delivering the new curriculum, who cannot cope with the growing knowledge could not manage the growing complex educational system. Therefore, teachers should be retrained to cope with the growing knowledge.

   In-service training should be organised to retain and re-orient teachers about the different subjects and new curriculum delivery.

   Teacher training should be an ongoing process to maintain an up·date their knowledge.

   Teachers should be provided with regular professional support.

9. Assessment and examination are essential techniques for monitoring learner's performance. However, it will have a negative impact if we use them as a means of ensuring that the curriculum is covered. This will encourage vote-memorisation if teachers tend to focus their teaching to such examinations.

   To transform the present examination systems into an effective tool to improve the quality and relevance of education:

   - Classroom based continuous assessment tools should be developed which are intended to develop the creativity, problem-solving etc... skills of students.
   - Summative assessment should also be done by giving examination at year-end.
   - Teachers should be trained to become familiar with the techniques required to conduct school-based assessment and examinations.

10. Involve all players and partners, each in his/her field, with his/her share of responsibility; families, parent-teacher associations of nationals living and working elsewhere, educational personnel, administrators, managers, trade unions and students.

    Material, financial, moral, spiritual, etc...contribution. SELF-SUFFICIENCY.

11. Learning, making people learn, learning to learn thinking methods, working methods, alone, in group, through mutual aid, assistance, etc...AUTONOMY

Theme III:* *Managing of Transition and Innovation in Secondary Education.

6. Conclusions and recommendations

Problem area	*Highlights on International trends*	*Issues*	*Recommandations*
Transition	• International trends in transition and innovations (a) Gross enrolment rate in sub-saharan Africa is generally low but is on the increase in average. It is currently at between 20-25%. (b) The Government budget allocations for education in sub-saharan Africa is at an average of 15-20%. This is not enough for African Countries. (c) Developed countries spend a lot more per primary school pupil per year than the African Countries South of the Sahara.	1. Inadequate resources to implement synchronized planning for primary and secondary education provision	1. Capacity building for education, planners, teachers, head teachers/ principals and school boards 2. Prioritization of Education funding in the Government Budgets—both local and central governments 3. Increased budgetary allocation 4. Solicit additional cooperating partner funding for secondary education 5. Improvement and expansion of physical infrastructure 6. Improvement and expansion of EMIS to enhance fiscal planning skills

(Contd.)

Problem area	Highlights on International trends	Issues	Recommandations
Transition	(d) Similarly pupils spend at the lower level 800-1000 hours in school in Europe while in many countries in Africa they spend less in a year. (e) There is more vocational education in Europe than General Education while in Africa it is mostly not the case.	2. Inadequate and irrelevant curriculum (The curriculum is narrow and more academic oriented—not addressing the requirements of the individual and the market	7. Review of current curriculum with a view to broaden it to accommodate different learner interests, needs and respond to both local and international needs. High quality curriculum should be upheld.
	(f) Management of secondary education is mostly decentralised in advanced economies while in many of the African countries, there is still a lot of centralization of Management.	3. Rigid and discriminatory highly selective examinations testing only cognitive skills	8. Review of the Examination System so as to accommodate larger participation in the next level.
	(g) Leading trends in primary education is on a rapid increase (h) Leading trends in secondary education is little and is on a slow increase.	4. Highly Centralised school ownership and management (in many countries Central Government owns and manages most schools, hence expansion is slow)	9. Gradual and cautions decentralization of ownership and management to local authorities/ communities under instituted mechanisms for Quality Control

(Contd.)

Problem area	Highlights on International trends	Issues	Recommandations
	• The Mauritian Case: (a) There is an increased transition from primary to secondary education, standing at 74% in Form 1. (b) Noted big gaps in cohorts progression e.g. 60% in Form 5 and 27% in Form 6. (c) Improvement of transition through • Addressing the issue of type and quality of examinations • Pedagogical reforms • Infrastructural improvements	5. Absence/inadequate guidance, counseling and appropriate information on secondary school options, tertiary institutions and world of work. (Lack of visions, missions and objectives/directions on the part of the learner) 6. Inadequate school places (slow, in some cases stagnant expansion of secondary education provision compared with population	10. Improve teacher skills to provide the required counseling and guidance to pupils and students • Call upon other stakeholder's ministries- e.g. Labour, Works, Youth and Culture, Community Development, Health, Agriculture, Mass Media, Companies and Industry to participate in information provision and dissemination to schools.

(Contd.)

Problem area	Highlights on International trends	Issues	Recommandations
	(d) Plans to manage reforms through • structural changes • monitoring; establishment of benchmarks for pedagogy, curriculum implementation and new management styles. (e) Professional development • Teachers • Rectors • Trainers (f) Research to provide warning signals and suggesting early and timely interventions (g) Manage public opinion	growth and primary education expansion	11. Increase infrastructure for secondary education by building more classroom and new schools. 12. Use of Double Shift System where possible 13. Provide secondary education through evening classes using existing school facilities and trained field teachers. 14. Provide secondary education through distance learning through correspondence 15. Use Electronic media 16. Put Population management policies in place and implementation them.
		7. High drop put rate at secondary education	Institute multigrade teaching/ learning approach to improve participation and retention (reduce dropout).

In view of the pertinent problems of transition caused by inadequate resources, poorly motivated teachers, inadequate curriculum, low management capacities, absence of appropriate education management and operational information systems, it is recommended that in-depth studies be undertaken in selected countries focusing on the highlighted issues.

Depending on the outcomes and findings Project proposals be prepared for funding.

Establish a mechanism to enhance education information flow among African countries so as to enable, learning from successful practice elsewhere.

Theme IV: Access, Equity and Quality

Equity and quality

7. General conclusions and recommendations

(a) Access:

1. One of the Reasons for the low participation rate in Education is due to lack of basic infrastructure. This cannot be left only to governments and foreign aid. The communities should be fully involved in the school management in partnership with other stakeholders i.e the private sector and religious institutions.

2. Another reason for low participation is that many schools are too far away from the communities. Therefore bring the schools to the communities as much as possible so that pupils would not have to travel/walk long distances.

3. Alternative modes of delivery of secondary education should be explored e.g. Distance and mobile schools for nomads should be planned and used extensively.

(b) Equity:

4. Schools beginning from the primary should be gender friendly (i.e. such as building separate toilet

for girls, issuing text books etc.) and affirmative actions such as helping poor girls, financially, giving tutorial for academically weak girls and relaxing the selection criteria for entry into secondary schools should be promoted.

5. Sensitise parents on the importance and need to send their children especially daughters to school and giving the daughters enough time to study at home by sharing the household chores evenly among the family members (siblings).

6. The issue of early motherhood, HIV/AIDS and other STI should be addressed at school in collaboration with other stakeholders such as the parents, the church and community leaders.

7. There exists strong disparities/inequalities between rural and urban Secondary schools. Governments should therefore take into account in the planning and development of secondary schools some of the following: adequate infrastructure, housing for teachers, libraries/laboratories etc, Enabling environment to encourage pupils not only to go to school but also to stay,

(c) Quality:

8. The Role of Teacher is very important in Quality delivery and governments should not lose sight of this.

9. To achieve this, distance learning should be encouraged to enable teachers to improve on their knowledge skills and competencies to be able to cope with globalisation.

10. It is also necessary to review the concept of quality and to look into it in terms of living together, providing life skills, good citizenship and the use of ICT to be able cope with the demands of global change.

11. All these should be taken into consideration when renewing or reforming the curriculum in the training of teachers.

12. To ensure success in Quality education all major stakeholders should be brought on board and these are, the state, regional, local/district authorities various groups and associations, the private sector and more importantly parents, teachers, and the learners themselves.

Theme V: The reform of secondary education and teacher training

8. Conclusions and recommendations

A. Issues:

1. Contested content.

   The content should reflect the reality of schools. For example, teachers should be trained in skills like; handling large numbers, multi-grade teaching and double shift teaching.

2. Preparation (Process of training teachers)

   Not based on good practice and action research. In some countries it is fragmented... not cost efficient and cost effective. People who prepare curriculum are not the same people who teach the content.

3. Student teachers—last resort to teach, some don't meet minimum requirements example SA closing colleges.

4. Motivation/Retention—Teacher are paid relatively low. Therefore they are not committed to teaching

5. Attribution due to a number of factors: HIV/AIDS and Natural death Early retirement

6. Given the EFA demands how do we produce adequate quality teachers is a population with a large number of school going children requires more teachers in order to reduce PTR.

7. Financing teacher education.

8. Definition of a conceptual framework or how to train teachers.

9. There is lack of empirical research on teacher education.

B. Recommendations:

10. Stakeholders should participate in suggesting what should be in the curriculum. Should be for all, civic education human rights education, etc. What does the society feels?

11. The methodology of training should be based on good practice and action research.

12. Restructuring teacher education so that we can have all the concerned cadres together e.g. curriculum developer, inspectors of schools, teachers, lecturers, etc

13. Devise strategies that will attract people who would be committed to Teacher education like:

 (a) improving terms and conditions of service;

 (b) national awards; and.

 (c) attractive salaries.

14. Develop strategies on HIV/AIDS epidemic:

 (a) sensitisation/prevention of HIV/AIDS;

 (b) replacement of teachers.

15. Designing different models of training teachers to meet the EFA demands e.g. Keith models.

16. Increase budgetary allocations to teacher education.

17. There is a need to agree on a conceptual framework on teaching contents in schools... Teacher training institutions.

18. There is need for further researcher on teacher education issues in Africa.

19. Encourage distance education as a modality to reach as many teachers as possible.

20. Revisit the structure of incentives to teachers as follows:
    - Teachers should be allowed... Encouraged to up-grade.
    - Invite or send them to international/ national seminars, workshops and study tours.
21. Provide in instructional materials like Teachers Handbook to teachers for personal use.
22. Introduce accelerated in-service teacher training programmes to meet the demand of teachers. Capacity building for head teachers should...

Oman Ministry of Education. (2002). *Recommendations of the National Seminar on Secondary Education*. Muscat, 1-3 April.

1. Reform of Education

1. Islamic ideology, values of the society and the Omani cultural identity shall be the base for the Reform of Education.
2. An Education Reform Committee would be formed

2. Curricula

Recommendations of the National Seminar on Secondary Education Held in Muscat from 1/4 to 3/4/2002

Reform of Education

1. Islamic ideology, values of the society and the Omani cultural identity shall be the base for the Reform of Education.
2. An Education Reform Committee would be formed to include concerned parties from Ministries and different institutions to set up policies and approve plans and programmes so as to enhance interaction between educational sector and individuals on the one hand and concerned parties and the society.

3. Linkage should be made between Basic Education Programmes and Secondary Education on the one hand and the requirements of secondary education, higher education and the labour market on the other hand.
4. Emphasize quality of education through development of methods and tools that help in improving internal and external competencies in the learning process.
5. Provide school buildings with all facilities that fulfill the objectives of the reform process.
6. International, regional and local expertise and studies will be consulted to enrich the reform of education.
7. The latest resources of knowledge will be adopted in the learning-teaching process.
8. Increase actual learning time in the school day as well as in the academic year in a way that suits fulfilment of desired goals.
9. Coordinate with parties concerned with employment and Omanisation to follow up the outcomes of the reform of education with regard to levels of knowledge and skills required for local manpower on the one hand and employment policies in labour market on the other hand.
10. Emphasize the role of the media in serving the educational process.
11. Enhance personal initiatives in improvement of education.

Curricula

1. Reform would be carried out in a comprehensive way that includes human resource development, facilities and educational requirements. In addition to that curricula will be reformed and developed

in order to accommodate the needs and requirements of the present era. Continuous financial support to education should be provided.

2. Design curricula on technology and technological tools.
3. Activate learning activities and link them to curricula and provide all necessary human and other resources to these activities, as they are essential in building the personality of the student.
4. Reform strategies of evaluation and assessment through finding alternatives other than tests and examinations. Continuous assessment should be implemented.
5. Attention should be paid to traditional Omani handicrafts and heritages and consider them as practical aspects that can have economic returns.
6. Decrease emphasis on the school textbook as a main source of knowledge.
7. Adopt modern and versified teaching methods.
8. Continuous evaluation of all aspects and areas of education should simultaneously accompany the reform process.
9. More care should be given to curricula development through conducting and publishing field studies and researches for public benefit and use.
10. Establish educational evaluation and assessment center and assign an authorized party to take care of such center.

School Administration

1. Adopt decentralisation in the management of secondary education.

2. Set up criteria for selection of administrative cadre of secondary education. Assignments and roles of such cadre should be clearly identified.
3. Emphasize the concept of efficient school administration that utilizes modern administrative techniques and human and other resources available to meet the desired objectives.

Teachers

1. Provide professional development programmes for teachers and for all who are involved in the educational reform process. Needs and facilities required should be taken into consideration and implementation mechanisms should be set up to follow the outcomes and effects of training.
2. Reconsider training programmes of teachers who will teach in grades eleven and twelve in accordance with the requirements of the reform through coordination between the Ministry and institutions concerned.
3. Improve the working and social conditions of teachers.
4. Decrease number of periods taught by the teacher and the senior teacher per week, and not assign them any administrative tasks so they can be able to carry out their teaching roles efficiently.
5. Reconsider basis for selection of trainee teachers in admission at colleges of education. Percentage obtained at the general secondary certificate exams will not be the only factor admission.
6. Provide the existing training centers with highly qualified personnel and enough facilities to meet the requirements of reform of education at grades eleven and twelve. New training centers should be opened in different regions of the country.

Students

1. Focus should be made on promotion of higher order skills and other mental abilities that helps the student to be productive and creative in academic life and in world of work.
2. Focus on students' guidance programmes and training of specialists in the guidance field, and provide all facilities that activate such programmes in the field.
3. Decrease class sizes.
4. Diversify school subjects for grades eleven and twelve in accordance with student's interests and aptitudes, and in the light of the requirements of social and economic development of the country and the diversification of the environment.
5. Involvement of society in setting school discipline procedures as students are in a critical age at this stage of their lives.

The Private Sector

1. Activate the role of the private sector in the reformed educational system.
2. Alignment of the reform programme with the latest developments and changes that occur at the local, regional and international levels on one hand, and the characteristics of the Basic Education system on the other hand.

Meetings and Seminars

1. Activate the outcomes of meetings, workshops and be utilized in planning present and future plans in away that meet and fulfill the desired objectives and targets.
2. Design specific mechanisms to implement the recommendations of the national seminar on secondary education.

III. Conference Programmeme

Secondary Education Reform Conference on the Reform of Secondary Education: Secondary Education for a Better Future-Trends, Challenges and Priorities

Sultante of Oman

Muscat
22-24 December 2002

Secondary Education for a Better Future: Trends, Challenges, and Priorities
An International Conference

22-24 December 2002, Al Bustan Palace Hotel
Muscat, Sultanate of Oman

Sunday 22.12.02

8:00-9:00am **Foyer**	**Registration**
9:00-10:00am **Oman Hall**	**Opening Ceremony** Speech by HE Minister of Education Speech by HE DG UNESCO Speech by HE DG Arab Bureau of Education for the Gulf States Short film
10:00-11:00am	**Break**
11:00-11:30am **Oman Hall**	**Introduction** *Sultanate of Oman- a Position Statement: Results of the National Conference "Education for a Better Future"* * Keynote: HE Dr. Fawzia Nasser Al-Farsi, Under Secretary for Education and Curricula, Sultanate of Oman Chairperson: HE Mohamed Al-Tobi Rapporteur: Dr. Said Al-Kitani
11:30am-12:00n **Oman Hall**	**Theme *A:* Re-defining Secondary Education for the 21st century: Why Change is Essential?** *Secondary education reform and expansion in the light of Education or All (EFA) and the Dakar Framework for Action*

	* Keynote: HE Koïchiro Matsuura, Director-General, UNESCO Chairperson: HE. Dr. Fawzia Al-Farsi Rapporteur: Dr. Abdullah Ambusaidi
12:15-1:30pm	**Concurrent Seminars**
Oman Hall	*Topic A, 1: Aligning the objectives and functions of Secondary Education to the new realities of the 21st century*
Presenter# 1	Prof. Bill Mulford, Director of Leadership for Learning Research Group, Faculty of Education, University of Tasmania, Australia: "Aligning the objectives and functions of Secondary Education to the realities of the 21st Century"
Presenter# 2	Dr. Badr Al-Oteibi, Arab Bureau of Education for the Gulf States, Kingdom of Saudi Arabia: "United Secondary School"
Presenter# 3	Dr. Ian Hill, International Baccalaureate Organisation, Geneva, Switzerland: "International Baccalaureate programmes: Curriculum model for National Secondary Education in the 21st Century". Chairperson: Dr. Wataru lwamoto Rapporteur: Mr. Iqbal Al-Balushi
Gulf Oman Hall	*Topic A, 2: Major challenges and dilemmas that face Secondary Education now and in the future, and the role of reform in meeting these challenges and dilemmas*
Presenter# 1	Dr. Abdulaziz Al-Rweis, Director of Curricular Development Department, Ministry of Education, Kingdom of Saudi Arabia: "A proposed model for development of Secondary Education: A flexible approach"
Presenter# 2	Dr. Mubarak Al-Hashmy, College of Education, Sultan Qaboos University,

	Sultanate of Oman: "Challenges facing secondary education at present and in the future"
Presenter# 3	Dr. Earle Warnica, Assessment Consultant, Ministry of Education, Sultanate of Oman: "A model for secondary education in The Sultanate of Oman: What happens after ten year of Basic Education"
	** Paper for distribution, submitted by Mr. Alan Patterson: "Secondary Education for a better future: Trends, Challenges and Priorities"
	** Paper for distribution, submitted by Mr. Hamoud Al-Harthy, College of Education, Sultan Qaboos University, Sultanate of Oman: "Globalisation and the necessity of educational reform in the Sultanate of Oman"
	Chairperson: Mr. Habeeb Al-Riyami
	Rapporteur: Mr. Hamed Al-Busaidi
Mazoon Hall	*Topic A, 3: Building on strengths and weaknesses: Priority areas for reform*
Presenter# 1	Dr. Victor Billeh, Director of UNESCO Regional Office, Beirut, Lebanon: "Building on strengths and weaknesses: Priority areas for reform of secondary education in the Arab States Region"
Presenter# 2	Mr. Mario Abela, Victoria Department of Education and Training, Victoria, Australia: "Imperatives for educational reform in secondary schooling and the Victorian response"
Presenter# 3	Dr. Salih Ulaymaat, Faculty of Education, Yarmouk University, Hashemite Kingdom of Jordan: "The educational system in globalisation era"
	Chairperson: Dr. Arif Attari
	Rapporteur: HH Sayidda Amaal Al-Said

Qurrayat Hall	*Topic B, 1 (a) AND Topic C. 5: World practices in dealing effectively with major dilemmas, such as Balancing Vocational and Academic Education AND Meeting the Needs of Post Secondary Education (Academic and Vocational)*
Presenter# 1	Dr. Abdullah Bubtana, Director of UNESCO Regional Office, Doha, State of Qatar: "Articulation and coherence between Secondary and Higher Education"
Presenter# 2	Ms. Aisha Al-Harthy, College of Education, Sultan Qaboos University, Sultanate of Oman: "Vocational Secondary Education: Success factors"
Presenter# 3	Squadron Leader Yahya Al-Rawahi, Royal Air Force of Oman, Sultanate of Oman: "Developing high-flying air force personnel: The challenges of matching Secondary Education outputs with the operational requirements of the Royal Air Force of Oman"
	Chairperson: HE Murtadha Hassan Ali
	Rapporteur: Ms Siddiqa Abdulmajeed
Tiwi Hall	**Topic B, 1(b):** World Practices in dealing effectively with major dilemmas, such as: Emphasising Knowledge & Cognitive Skills or Behavioural & Life Skills:
Presenter# 1	Dr. Sonia Bahri, Chief of the Section for General Secondary Education UNESCO: "Emphasising knowledge and cognitive skills or behavioural and life skills"
Presenter# 2	Dr. May Moore, LRCs Advisor, Ministry of Education, Sultanate of Oman: "The role and importance of LRC Information Literacy Skills Curriculum in the cognitive development of Secondary students"
Presenter# 3	Mr. Mohamed Al-Kiyumi, Secondary School Assistant Principal, Batinah South,

	Ministry of Education, Sultanate of Oman: "Developing innovative thinking for secondary students: Effective model for change: Chairperson: Dr. Hamad Al-Hammami Rapporteur: Mr. Ali Al-Balushi
1:30-3:00pm	**Lunch**
3:00-4:00pm **Oman Hall**	**Theme B: Effective New Models for Secondary Education in the 21st Century: The Focus for Change** * Keynote: Prof. J.S. Rajput, Director of National Council of Educational Research and Training (NCERT), India: "Effective new models for secondary education in the 21st Century: Focus on Change" Chairperson: HE Dr. Rawya Al-Busaidi Rapporteur: Dr. Muna Al-Jardani
4:15-5:15pm	**Concurrent Seminars**
Oman Hall	*Topic B, 2: Building better curriculum models*
Presenter# 1	Dr. Ken Shaw, University of Exeter, United Kingdom: "What the UK learned from the National Curriculum on Secondary Education"
Presenter# 2	Prof. Hayat Diyen, English Department, University of Mohamed Premier, Kingdom of Morocco: "The Reform of Secondary Education in the Arab World: Challenges and prospects"
Presenter# 3	Mr. Man Mohan Joshi, Principal of the Indian School, Muscat, Sultanate of Oman: "Futurising the transaction of curriculum" Chairperson: Dr. Cecilia Braslavsky Rapporteur: Ms Amal Al-Kiyumi
Tiwi Hall	*Topic B, 3: Best Practices in Assessment and strategic ways of changing methods of assessment:*

Presenter# 1	Mr. David Griffiths, Scottish Qualifications Authority, United Kingdom, presently seconded as Assessment Consultant, Ministry of Education, Sultanate of Oman: A series of checks and balances: Creating a quality assessment for certification system in Secondary Education"
Presenter# 2	Dr. Hanan Innabi, School of Education, United Arab Emirates University, United Arab Emirates: "Assessing critical thinking in Secondary School Instruction for Accountability: A need for rubrics" Chairperson: Dr. Abdullah Al-Sarmi; Rapporteur: Mr. Rashid Al-Hinai
Mazoon Hall	*Topic B, 4: Application of educational technologies*
Presenter #1	Dr. B. Kotsik, UNESCO Institute for Information Technologies in Education (IITE); "ICT Application in Secondary Education: Main trends, challenges and priorities"
Presenter# 2	Dr. Said Al-Rabiey, Deputy Director General, Directorate of Colleges of Education, Ministry of Higher Education, Sultanate of Oman: "Technology Integration in Secondary Education"
Presenter# 3	Dr. K. Ramachandrachar, Retired Professor, India: "Cyberspace use in Education: Transition tasks ahead and some perceptions of challenge" Chairperson: Dr. Moosa Al-Kindy Rapporteur: Mr. Yahya Al-Sarmi
Quarrayat Hall	*Topic B, 5: Career Guidance and Youth Counselling*
Presenter# 1	Prof. W.A. Borgen, Director, International Association for Counselling (IAC), Department of Educational and

	Counselling Psychology and Special Education, University of British Columbia, Vancouver, Canada: "Youth Counselling and Career Guidance"
Presenter# 2	Ms Deidre Teeling, National University of Ireland, Ireland: "The Irish Experience: Guidance and Counselling as part of the secondary school programme" Chairperson: Dr. Taifoor Albilli Rapporteur: Ms Suad Al-Fori
Gulf Oman Hall	*Topic B, 6: Routes to Cost Effectiveness*
Presenter# 1	HE Dr. Thuwabya Al-Barwani, Undersecretary, Ministry of Social Development, Sultanate of Oman: "Bridging the gap between Secondary Education, Tertiary Education, and the World of Work"
Presenter# 2	Dr. I. Kitaev, Programme Specialist (Educational Costs, Finance, and Budgeting), IIEP-UNESCO: "Routes to cost-effectiveness" Chairperson: HE Salem Al-Maskri Rapporteur: Ms Zainab Al-Qasmi
5:15pm	End
8:00pm	**HE The Minister of Education Hosted Dinner for All Participants**

Monday 23.12.02

8:00-8:45am Workshops

Gulf Oman Hall	**# 1: Mr. Don Stenson, Harcourt International, United States of America: "Helping science students become better critical thinkers for a better future"** **Chairperson: Dr. Earle Warnica** **Rapporteur: Ms Intisaar Ambusaidi**

Tiwi Hall	# 2: Ms. Jan Ellis, Marketing Executive, VT Careers Management, United Kingdom: "Using ICT and Careers Software to help young people make informed career decisiohs" Chairperson: Dr. May Moore Rapporteur: Mr. Hamed Al-Busaidi
9:00-10:30am	*Panel: Sultanate of Oman Stakeholder Perspectives*
Oman Hall	
Presenter# 1	Student representative- Miss Khatimah Al-Rusheidi
Presenter# 2	Parent representative- HE Salim Al-Ghatami
Presenter# 3	Teacher representative- Mr. Ahmed AJ-Mu'adi
Presenter# 4	Principal representative- Ms Aida Al-Jamali
Presenter# 5	Business representative- Ms Salwa Abdulamir Chairperson: HE Rajha Abdulameer Rapporteur: Ms Aisha Al-Harthy
10:30am	Break
11:00am-12:00n	**Theme C: Strategies for Successful Implementation of Reform:**
Oman Hall	**Practical Blueprints.** *Keynote: Ms. Carol Bates, Principal and Chief Executive, Harris City Technology College, United Kingdom: Chairperson: HE Dr. Thuwayba Al-Barwani Rapporteur: Dr. Ali Al-Shuely
12:15-1:15pm	**Concurrent Seminars**
Oman Hall	*Topic C, 1: The role of family and parents' involvement in strengthening community efforts to improve performance in secondary education*

Presenter# 1	Ms Joy de Leo, VP Asia-Pacific Network for International Education and Values Education, Australia: The role of family and parents' involvement in strengthening community efforts to improve performance in secondary education"
Presenter# 2	Mr. Ali Al-Habsi, Parents' Association, Shariqiya North, Sultanate of Oman: "Role of parents' group in developing education"
Presenter# 3	Mr. Seif Al-Nueimi, Parents' Association, Dhahira North, Sultanate of Oman: "Developing Secondary Education in Oman"
	Chairperson: Dr. Said Al-Rubeiy
	Rapporteur: Mr. Ali Al-Balushi
Gulf Oman Hall	*Topic C, 2: Taking into account student needs*
Presenter# 1	Dr. Zhou Nanzhao, Coordinator and Senior Programme Specialist, AIPED, UNESCO, Bangkok, Thailand: "Promoting Secondary Education for the Diversified Learning Needs of the Young: Challenges, Policy Reforms and Innovative Practices in Asia-Pacific Region"
Presenter# 2	Dr. Alireza Jamshidnejad, Head of Iranian School Health Group, Islamic Azad University of Dezful, Republic of Iran: "The organisational health and deputies' job stress in Secondary Schools"
	Chairperson: Dr. Sonia Bahri
	Rapporteur: Mr. Hanan Bait Obidoon
Mazoon Hall	*Topic C, 3: Appropriate Ways of Involving the Private and Public Sectors AND Topic C, 4: Addressing Labour Market Demands*
Presenter# 1	Dr. Kurt Hoffman, Director, Shell Foundation, London, United Kingdom:

	"Insights from outside the classroom: Experience and insights from non-traditional methods of training and education world-wide"
Presenter# 2	Dr. Juma Al-Ghailani; Oman Chamber of Commerce and Industry: "Quality of Secondary Education and labour market requirements" Chairperson: HE Rahila Riyami Rapporteur: Ms Intisaar Ambusaidi
Qurrayat Hall	*Topic C, 6: New trends in the pre-service and in-service preparation of teachers for the reform of secondary education*
Presenter# 1	Dr. Gari Donn, General Secretariat of the Commonwealth, London, United Kingdom: "The role of Oman's Colleges of Education in the implementation of reform: The case of the Basic Education Curriculum"
Presenter# 2	Dr. Salha Issan, College of Education, Sultan Qaboos University, Sultanate of Oman: "Teachers' preparation and qualification: A futuristic outlook"
Presenter# 3	Dr. Abdullah Al-Tobi, College of Education, Nizwa, Ministry of Higher Education, Sultanate of Oman: "How to reform pre-service teacher education programmes in Oman in order to meet the requirement of the reformed general education in science!" Chairperson: Dr. Monique Fouiloux Rapporteur: Mr. Seif Al-Hadhrami
Tiwi Hall	*Topic C, 7: The critical importance of leadership at all levels in managing Educational Change*
Presenter# 1	Prof. R. Bolem, University of Cardiff, United Kingdom: "The critical importance of leadership at all levels in managing educational change"

Presenter# 2	Dr. Wajeha Al-Ani, College of Education, Yarmouk University, Hashemite Kingdom of Jordan: "Effective Instructional Strategy: A suggested matrix" Chairperson: Dr. Ahmed Al-Hinai Rapporteur: Mr. Nabhan Al-Lamki
1:15-2:45pm	Lunch
2:45-3:15pm	**Report from the Consultancy Study on The Reform of Grades 11**
Oman Hall	**and 12 in the Sultanate of Oman**
Presenter:	Dr. Sana Al-Balushi, Director, Technical Office for Studies and Development, Ministry of Education, Sultanate of Oman Chairperson: HE Dr. Ali Fakhro Rapporteur: Dr. Salma Al-Humeidy
3:25-4:25pm	**Theme D: Practices in Evaluating the Success of Reform**
Oman Hall	*Keynote: Prof. W.J. Popham, Professor Emeritus, University of California and Los Angeles, United States of America: "The School Reform Evaluator: Appraiser or Improver?" Chairperson: HE Dr. Ali Fakhro Rapporteur: Dr. Salma Al-Humeidy
4:40-5:40pm	**Concurrent Seminars**
Gulf Oman Hall	*Topic C, 8: Government Approaches to Policy and Practice*
Presenter# 1	Dr. Emily Vargas-Baron, Director, Institute for Reconstruction of International Security through Education (RISE), United States of America: "Participatory policy planning processes for Secondary and Youth Education"
Presenter# 2	Dr. Mohamed Al-Duraig, Sohar College of Education, Ministry of Higher Education, Sultanate of Oman:

	"Educational Partnership in Secondary Education" Chairperson: HE Dr. Mohammed Al-Dhahab Rapporteur: HH Sayidda Amaal Al-Said
Oman Hall	**Topic D, 1: Accountability: Setting and meeting standards**
Presenter# 1	Dr Wataru Iwamoto, Director, Division of Secondary, Technical, and Vocational Education, UNESCO: "Accountability: Setting and meeting standards"
Presenter# 2	Ms. Zainab Al-Qasmi, Deputy Head of English Language Department, Higher College of Technology, Ministry of Manpower, Sultanate of Oman: "Effects of evaluation and inspection on standards of education" Chairperson: Dr. Hamed Al-Dhahab Rapporteur: Ms Maryam Al-Nabhani
Mazoon Hall	**Topic D, 2: Maximising Access, Opportunity and Completion Rates**
Presenter# 1	Ms Susan Pearson, School of Education, University of Leeds, United Kingdom: Academic Excellence within inclusive settings"
Presenter# 2	Dr. Steven Bakker, Director, Business Development, Educational Testing Services (ETS) Europe, The Netherlands: "PISA from 2000-2003 proficiency in Math and Science" Chairperson: HE Ali Al-Mahrouqy Rapporteur: Mr. Yahya Al-Sarmi
Qurrayat Hall	**Topic D, 3: Measuring Improvement in Educational Outcomes**
Presenter# 1	Paper written by Prof. V. Chinapah, Division for Promotion of Quality Education, UNESCO, to be presented by Dr. Sulieman Sulieman, UNESCO

	Regional Office Beirut: "Measuring improvement in learning outcomes"
Presenter# 2	Mr. Said Al-Adawi, Deputy Director General of Curriculum, Ministry of Education, Sultanate of Oman: "Collaborative planning for school improvement"
	Chairperson: Dr. Salha Issan
	Rapporteur: Ms Hanan Bait-Obidoon
Tiwi Hall:	**Topic D, 4: Examining Indicators of Capacity Building at the School and Community Level**
Presenter# 1	Dr Roger-Francois. Gauthier, Inspector General of Education and Research Administration, France: "Finding an equilibrium between the external and internal evaluations of secondary schools"
Presenter# 2	Dr. Gillian Plummer, School Evaluation Expert, Ministry of Education, Sultanate of Oman: "A better future for all"
	Chairperson: Dr. Nariman Juma
	Rapporteur: Ms Fathiya Al-Maawaly
5:40pm	End
Tuesday	**24.12.02**
9:00-10:00am	**Theme E: Sharing New Ideas for Change**
Oman Hall	*Keynote: HE Dr. Ali Fakhro, Kingdom of Bahrain: "The future of Secondary Education"
	Chairperson: HE Dr. Ahmed Al-Ghazali
	Rapporteur: Dr. Salha Issan
10:15-11:15am	Concurrent sessions: Sharing Ideas by topic or country
Gulf Oman Hall	Sharing ideas on Curriculum:
Presenter# 1	Dr. Nancy Cerezo, Assistant Professor, College of Education, Zayed University, United Arab Emirates: "Problem-based

	learning in the middle school: Perceptions of at-risk students"
Presenter# 2	Dr. Abdullah Ambusaidi, College of Education, Sultan Qaboos University, Sultanate of Oman: "Teaching strategies for Secondary Education"
	Chairperson: Dr. Mohamed Aluqda
	Rapporteur: Mr Rashid Al-Hinai
Oman Hall	**Sharing Ideas on Curriculum:**
Presenter# 1	Dr. Nor Aisha Buang, College of Education, National University of Malaysia, Malaysia: "Towards building a better curriculum model for Science Education in Malaysian Secondary Schools: A scientist entrepreneurial approach"
Presenter# 2	Dr. Suleiman Al-Qaderi, Department of Educational Sciences, Al-Albayt University, Hashemite Kingdom of Jordan: "The status of Science Education in the Secondary School, its challenges and the role of epistemology and metacognition in its reform"
Presenter# 3	Dr. Reda Abu-Elwan, College of Education, Sultan Qaboos University, Sultanate of Oman: "A proposed model for the content of the Mathematics Curricular in Secondary Education in the light of the current professional requirements"
	Chairperson: Dr. Muna Al-Jaradani
	Rapporteur: Mr. Nabhan Al-Lamki
Mazoon Hall	**Sharing Ideas on Labour Market and Manpower Issues:**
Presenter# 1	Sayyida Zakiya Al-Busaidi, President, Oman Womens' Association, Muscat, Sultanate of Oman: "A proposed formula for development of Secondary Education

	in the light of trends of Vocational Schools in the Sultanate of Oman"
Presenter# 2	Group Captain Hilal Al-Hinai, Royal Air Force of Oman, Sultanate of Oman: "Challenges facing technical education in the Royal Air Force of Oman"
Presenter# 3	Ms Zainab Al-Qasmi, Deputy Head of English Language Department, Higher College of Technology, Ministry of Manpower, Sultanate of Oman: "To what extent are national educational systems considered as the main gate to economic competition?" Chairperson: HE Aflah Al-Rawahi Rapporteur: Ms Suad Al-Fori
Qurrayat Hall	**Sharing Ideas from Different Countries:**
Presenter# 1	Sudan: Dr. Gasim Badri, Vice Chancellor, Ahfad University: "The current status of secondary education: Special focus on Sudan"
Presenter# 2	Kenya: Mr. Sam Mbure, Gakau Education Foundation: "Secondary School education in Africa- Tackling new challenges"
Presenter# 3	State of Qatar: Mr. Tariq Abdallah, Principal of the Scientific School Ministry of Education: "Reform of the Educational System of Qatar (The Scientific School Model)" Chairperson: Dr. Mohamed Al-Bandary Rapporteur: Mr. Seif Al-Hadhrami
Tiwi Hall	**Sharing Ideas from Different Countries:**
Presenter# 1	India: Mr. Ashok Ganguly, Chairman, Central Board of Secondary Education: "Re-defining secondary education for the 21st Century"
Presenter# 2	Kingdom of Bahrain: Mr. Nasser Mohamed Al-Sheikh, Director of

	Preparatory and Secondary Education, Ministry of Education: "New Effective models to reform secondary education in the Kingdom of Bahrain"
Presenter# 3	Uganda: Mr. Albert Byamugisha, Assistant Commissioner, Educational Planning, Ministry of Education and Sports: "Maximising access, opportunity, and completion rates regarding Secondary Education: The case of Africa and more specifically, Uganda"
	**Paper for distribution, submitted by Prof. Toji Tanaka, Institute of Education, University of Tsukuba, Japan: "The experience and perspective of the Japanese reform in Secondary Education: A dilemma between integration and differentiation of curriculum"
	Chairperson: HE Sheikh Amer Qattan
	Rapporteur: Ms Maryam Al-Nabhani
11:15am-12:15pm	Break
12:15-1:30pm	Final Session and Closing Ceremony
Oman Hall	Presentation of conference report and recommendations for secondary education reform.
	Chairperson: HE Dr. Ahmed Al-Jalali, Ambassador and Permanent Representative of Iran to UNESCO
	Rapporteurs-General: Prof. Bill Mulford; Dr. Said Al-Kitani
1.30-3:00pm	Lunch

IV. Speeches Presented at the Conference

1. His Excellency Yahya bin Saud bin Mansoor Al-Sulaimi, Minister of Education

In the name of Allah, Most Merciful and Compassionate,

Peace and Blessings Be Upon Muhammad and upon his kith and kin.

Your Highness, Sayyid Haitham bin Tareq Al Said, Minister of National Heritage and Culture,

Your Excellencies,

Your Excellency the Director General of UNESCO,

Your Excellencies the Members of the State Council and the A'Shurah Council,

Honourable Guests and Delegates:

> It is indeed a very pleasant opportunity for us to meet today to open the proceedings of the First International Conference on Secondary Education Reform. This conference is organised in cooperation with the United Nations Education, Science and Culture Organisation (UNESCO) to consider the trends, challenges and priorities of secondary education which should ensure a better future for our youth. The conference will also highlight how secondary education is a crucial stage in human resource planning and development.

I am pleased and honoured to welcome our participating guests who come from brotherly and friendly states to express their views and to share their expertise and experience in order to arrive at innovative answers for the reform and development of secondary education in the light of the intellectual, cultural, scientific, technological and economic changes that have emerged at the dawn of the third millennium.

Honourable Participants:

> The organisation of this conference has been inspired by the directives of His Majesty Sultan Qaboos bin Said who has called for the reform and development of education in the Sultanate so that it can match the rapid development of the country and so that school leavers will be fully prepared for the demands of this modern age and for future challenges. You are all aware how education plays an important role in all nations and indeed education is an effective tool for bringing about social change and is the obvious means for any national development. Secondary education, in particular, is at a crossroads which can lead in different directions to specialised and academic higher education, to technical and professional education or directly to the world of work.

The allocation of students to these pathways according to their state of readiness, their capabilities, their inclinations and their desires as well as on the basis of reasonable ratios which take into consideration both individual choices and the country's need for human resources in different areas, all this represents a serious intellectual challenge for you and calls for reviewing expertise and experience and for sharing views among the participants so that your conference can define the place of secondary education in the twenty-first century. The conference will also hopefully complete what has already been realized by other conferences held in recent years in this field and will determine appropriate models for secondary education and propose new implementation strategies, assessment methods and teacher training policies.

Honourable participants:

> This is the global vision for the reform of secondary education. We are fully confident that a forum of this kind, gathering as it does such as elite of thinkers and education experts from different parts of the world, will not close without attaining its expected goals and objectives.

To conclude, I should like to extend our warmest thanks to His Highness Sayyid Haitham bin Tareq Al Said, Minister of National Heritage and Culture for kindly presiding over this conference. I should also like to thank their Excellencies and the conference delegates for accepting our invitation and for participating in this learned event. We would take this opportunity to wish them a pleasant stay in the Sultanate of Oman as well as every success in achieving the conference objectives.

2. *His Excellency Koïchiro Matsuura, Director General of UNESCO*

Mr. Yahya bin Saud bin Mansoor Al-Sulaimi, Minister of Education,
Excellencies,
Distinguished Speakers and Participants,
Ladies and Gentlemen,

I am very pleased to be here once again in Oman to open this International Conference on 'Secondary Education for a Better Future: Trends, Challenges and Priorities', organised by the Government of Oman in collaboration with UNESCO. I would like to thank Mr Al-Sulaimi, the Minister of Education, for the kind and hospitable reception you have given me and for the excellent liaison that UNESCO's professional staff have enjoyed with the educational authorities of Oman in the preparation of this meeting. It is a real pleasure to be in your country once more.

This International Conference on Secondary Education is an important initiative which once again reveals the seriousness with which Oman is addressing its national educational development. It is commendable that Oman is locating that development within an international context of trends, good practices and experience that are an invaluable source of knowledge and insight. In this globalising age, good judgement and sound policy-making must draw upon processes of international comparison through which one can select the proven, the valid and the suitable.

As you may recall, in March 2001 I had the pleasure to open here in Oman the International Conference on "The University of the 21st Century", which UNESCO jointly organised with your country. In regard to last year's conference and today's occasion, I would like to congratulate the Government of Oman for these initiatives, which reflect a strong commitment to placing human resource development at the heart of all development. To this end, the improvement of all types and levels of education is essential.

Education is not only a basic right but is also an investment that pays economic, social and cultural dividends benefiting individuals and whole societies alike. Education, furthermore, is an instrument for forging national identity as well as for building national capacity. Indeed, education is a remarkable tool that is flexible and multi-purpose in character. But, in our rapidly changing world, it needs to be kept under constant review lest it becomes ill-adapted to new realities and ceases to perform its functions. Education must therefore be periodically renewed. It is gratifying to see that Oman recognises and understands these processes. The conference being opened today is a testament to Oman's appreciation of the fact that education is the answer but only so long as its questions are relevant and responsive to genuine needs.

I am pleased to note that Oman, which joined the Organisation in 1972, has always maintained excellent relations with UNESCO in all its fields of competence. As this conference shows, Oman is very much attuned to the mission and priorities of UNESCO. Indeed, I would like to congratulate you on the title of this conference— "Education for a better future" — as this is, in essence, UNESCO's 'raison d'être'. I understand that this same theme was the focus of a national symposium held here in April 2002, aimed at generating a national consensus on this subject. I believe that the Ministry of Education deserves great credit for its efforts to build a solid national agreement on the way forward for secondary education.

If basic education is the foundation of learning in modern societies, secondary education is the hinge on which many doors are hung. One door opens the chance to complete basic education; another door offers the opportunity to move forward to higher education; and yet another door opens the ways towards technical and vocational education. Adolescence is a time of opportunity but it is also a time or risk, and secondary education must be relevant to the problems that young people are facing now or will face in the future. These problems include those of drug abuse, HIV/AIDS, exclusion, discrimination and violence. To be relevant, secondary education must cultivate the kinds of values, attitudes, behaviours and skills that equip young people to handle the challenges of adulthood, citizenship and rapid economic, social, cultural and technological change.

Many countries are re-structuring their secondary education system and others are planning to do so. In all cases, innovation must be appropriate to local contexts and informed by others' experience. This is why UNESCO is focusing its action on the promotion of international policy dialogue and the exchange of information about innovative good practices.

Last year, UNESCO organised in Beijing an International Experts Meeting on 'Secondary Education in the 21st Century'. As a result, we have been better able to identify some key challenges and priority areas relating to secondary education reform, many of which, I am pleased to observe, are reflected in the themes and topics contained in the programme of this International Conference being held here in Oman. I will explore some of these matters shortly in my keynote speech on the theme of "Re-defining secondary education for the 21st century: Why change is essential", in the perspective afforded by Education for All and the Dakar Framework for Action.

The themes and issues you are to examine in this conference are truly important for they address, directly or indirectly, the formation of the next generations of young people, in whose hands all of our futures are entrusted. I wish you every success in your work.

Thank you

3. Dr. Said Al-Mulais, Director General of the Arab Bureau of Education for the Gulf States

In the name of Allah, Most Gracious, Most Merciful

Praise to God who has created Man and taught him speech. Peace and Blessings upon Mohammad, the best of all who learnt and taught, on His family and all His companions.

- Your Highness Haitham bin Tareq Al Said, Minister of Heritage and Culture,
- Your Excellency Dr. Koichiro Matsuura, Director General of UNESCO,

- Your Excellency Yahya bin Saud Al-Sulaimi, Minister of Education,
- Excellencies, Ladies and Gentlemen,

On this blessed day in Muscat, on the land of the Sultanate of Oman, which is thriving with its leadership and with its people, radiant with its present and history. My greetings filled with pride, consideration, esteem and admiration are addressed to His Majesty Sultan Qaboos bin Said who, thanks to His leadership, the Sultanate has achieved great strides, and with His wisdom the foundations of development have been laid down, making the prosperity of the Omani citizen a genuine objective around, which development plans have been designed on the land of this nation whose mountains stand high and rivers have become affluent, and which is proud of its children who are setting the example by their generosity and contribution, high ambition and loyalty, and by learning from science and knowledge whose paths have been opened for them and in which they have engaged with confidence.

Our greetings are also addressed to Mr. Koïchiro Matsuura, Director General of UNESCO. We pray God to help him in making education an instrument of rapprochement, a means of understanding, and a message of love, peace and brotherliness among mankind and in life.

Our sincere salutations also go to His Excellency Yahya bin Saud Al-Sulaimi, Minister of Education for the distinguished efforts generously expended in the field of education in the Sultanate, and for his constant support to the work of the Arab Bureau of Education of the Gulf States. Our greetings also addressed to his colleagues, men and women, who spare no efforts in serving the goals of the Bureau and encouraging its programmes and projects.

Your Highness, Honorable participants,

A few months ago we held here our National Conference on Secondary Education and followed its different sessions and activities with much interest. This conference had a deep impact on us in view of its goals, organisation, themes, conduct, results and recommendations. And here we are today gathered in this international conference, fully confident that its outcome and contribution will live up to our expectations and hopes and will be realistic and in keeping with the trends and challenges and auguring of what we have always been used to from the organisers of this conference.

Secondary education which has brought us together today will remain a deep concern of education for educators and researchers in view of the importance of this educational stage in the lives of our children who look forward to the future, aspire to rise very high, are keen on engaging in adventure and taking risks, and are anxious to unfold unknown knowledge, while their nations hope to ensure their participation in their development, achieving their goals and securing a decent living based on previously prepared developmental plans and programmes to match our children's aspirations or not.

As a matter of fact,. the problem of accommodating secondary education systems in our countries with the requirements of this educational stage lies in this difficult equation. Are we able to achieve this articulation? Can secondary education in our region become a tool for preparing a citizen immune and cemented with faith, equipped with science, good morals and dreams, capable of building oneself and participating in the construction of his or her society and nation?

Can our secondary education prepare our children to coexist with the challenges of today's world, with a future that has disturbed those who have looked up to it and kept awake those have been thinking about it?

Is our secondary education able to meet the aspirations contained in the famous report on education, that hidden treasure through which UNESCO has impacted the field of educational thought when it said that "Secondary education is the stage during which talents, in their diversity, should be disclosed and should prosper. Common elements of educational curricula (languages, science and general culture) should be enriched and modernised so as to encompass the increasing universal nature characterising phenomena as well as the need for understanding between cultures while using science for the sustainable development goals".

Can our secondary education make us feel happy one day to proudly raise the following motto: "Secondary school has succeeded"?

These many questions and concerns place on this conference the burden of finding the answers. Everybody is looking forward to the results of this conference, and we, at the Arab Bureau of Education of the Gulf States, are also awaiting its outcomes, while we are moving ahead to implement our programmes and our planned reforms in this field which is still a fertile area and requires further work and greater efforts and contribution.

All our greetings to the Ministry of Education in the Sultanate for constantly engaging in these important educational areas with potency and competence. Our greetings to the Ministry of Education for bringing together this distinguished gathering of experts, researchers and stakeholders whose deep thoughts, longstanding experience and sound views are needed by our secondary education system. So what do we plan to do? We will certainly do much on the land of Oman and under the guidance of His Majesty Sultan Qaboos bin Said.

May God grant full success to this Conference.

Thank you for your attention

4. ***His Excellency Mohammed bin Hamdan Al-Tobi, Under-Secretary for Educational Planning and Projects in the Ministry of Education***

In the name of Allah, Most Merciful, Most Compassionate,

Peace and Blessings Be Upon the Last of the Messengers, Muhammad, on His Kin and Kith.

Excellencies,
Honourable Guests,

We were very pleased to follow with much interest and attention the proceedings of your Conference throughout the past three days and learnt everything about the content of the lively presentations made here and which were characterised by seriousness, truth and clarity and reflected the richness of your experience and broad expertise in the field of education and knowledge.

We were indeed very pleased at your presence amongst us throughout the duration of the conference. The educational sphere has been honoured and uplifted by your attendance and your innovative thoughts. We thank you and highly appreciate the efforts made for the success of this event which sought to reach a common vision stemming from the fusion of diverse experience, broad expertise and innovative vision into a common direction heading towards a unified educational process seeking to achieve the expected outcome in terms of skills and knowledge.

We would like to thank you and express our gratitude to you for taking the burden of travelling, preparing the working papers, and for your lively and exciting presentation of these papers. While declaring the closing of this important educational conference, the Ministry of Education of the Sultanate of Oman would like to extend its warmest thanks and gratitude to you and to all those who have contributed to the planning, implementation and success of this commendable work. Our thanks also go to the United Nations Organisation for Education, Science and Culture, the Arab Bureau of Education in the Gulf States, to all the institutions and individuals who contributed either by their ideas, support to or presence at this educational event. The Ministry will always keep in mind your valuable participation for which it expresses its everlasting consideration and gratitude.

Excellencies,
Honourable Guest,

I would like to praise the final report issued by the conference and which will be considered as an important document by the Minisiry and which will be constantly referred to in its planning and follow up of the ongoing educational reform process. Much attention will be accorded to your recommendations as they will constitute the primary reference for the decision-makers at the Ministry of Education with respect to the reform of education in the post-basic education phase.

In conclusion, I would like to wish our guests a safe journey back to their countries and reaffirm to our fellow participants from the Sultanate that the Ministry will do its best to take account of all the outcomes of this conference and endeavour to put them into practice in fulfilment of their aspirations and ambitions.

We ask Allah Almighty to keep education as a message of peace to all nations and peoples, protect the whole world from every evil and danger, spread the blessing of peace and security on our country Oman, the land of peace under the leadership of the Man of peace, His Majesty Sultan Qaboos bin Said, may Allah protect Him and preserve Him.

Thank you for your attention.

5. Dr. Aziza Banani, Moroccan Ambassador to UNESCO and Chairwoman of the UNESCO Executive Council

In the name of Allah, Most Merciful, Most Compassionate

Excellencies,
Ladies and Gentlemen,

I would like to start my address by expressing my warmest thanks to His Excellency Yahya bin Saud Al-Sulaimi, Minister of Education in the brotherly Sultanate of Oman for kindly inviting me to participate in this international conference on the reform of secondary education which is held under the title of "Secondary Education for a Better Future". I also thank His Excellency for the warm welcome and generous hospitality we have received during the days spent here. I would like to take this opportunity to congratulate him as well as the participants for the results reached by our conference; thanks to the high level of the participants, excellent organisation and arrangements, not to mention the strong will for constructive dialogue and open-mindedness towards new and valuable ideas that we found among everybody.

I am also pleased to congratulate the Omani authorities for taking the initiative in organising this important conference and for the continuous efforts made to develop and reform the Sultanate's educational system. Last year, the Sultanate organised an international conference on higher education under the title: "The University of the Twenty-First Century", clearly attesting to the deep interest that this country places on the question of educational reform in every stage of the educational process, and the importance it accords to education which is the cornerstone of human resource development at a time we are entering straightforward into the knowledge-based society.

The basic task lying ahead of an organisation concerned with education, science and culture, such as UNESCO, consists in seeking the most appropriate ways for preparing the entire international community to engage in the age of an "educated world". This phase requires that the nations of the world, and particularly the developing nations, be prepared to engage in this competition which calls every nation to contribute what they can so as to survive and not to be left on the roadside. The first step required to bridge the gap between the developing nations and advanced countries lies in providing education to everyone. This is absolutely vital to secure a comprehensive knowledge and build the technical capabilities necessary for economic and social development. Education is a basic key to reducing the differences within each society and between nations, let alone that it is one of the priorities among human rights principles.

The function of education today goes beyond acquiring and piling up knowledge. Education is expected to build up personality, individual personality and social personality. The school is requested to produce a science seeker and graduate, a responsible citizen, a citizen in his or her own nation and an international citizen capable of responding to, interacting with and facing up to every challenge witnessed by our world, a world in the process of becoming a global village. This race, in which we engage with the new information age alongside with its information and communication technologies and fast-moving development, today enables mankind to achieve within a decade what it used to achieve in decades if not in centuries.

Thanks to this acceleration in innovation and production, mankind can achieve qualitative development which enables it to reach prosperity and well-being, especially in medicine and in combating severe diseases. But at the same time, it represents a threat for those societies that are unable to keep up with the pace of scientific and technological progress as long as these societies do not react and take the responsibility of addressing this challenge so that they may equip themselves with the necessary tools and skills and embark on the process of today's scientific civilisation. In order to build an educated society in an educated world, we must think of each of its stones, of each simple component of its construction. In the galaxy of knowledge, each mind is a star in itself and the minds of our children are the stones necessary for the construction of tomorrow's educated world. The more attention we accord to these talented and gifted minds and to their diverse expertise and knowledge, the more we contribute to opening up the gate of the future for our countries.

Education is expected to be an industrial laboratory for building tomorrow's society. According to the report of the International Committee for Education in the 21st Century, for education to fulfil its role in the edification of the knowledge-based society, it should be founded on four pillars that are crucial to the building up of modern personality: Education for Knowledge, Education for Work, Education for Living Together and Education for Being. From my point of view, we should not overlook a fifth principle, which must be considered in every educational policy, and which consists in encouraging the spirit of creativity. We deduce from these principles what has been deduced by the Committee chaired by Jacques Delors which stated that what is needed is to make human beings "friends of science" all their life long, and that there are no possible limits to knowledge. We may therefore say that the International Committee for Education in the 21st Century is in tune with what has been attributed to Socrates, the father of philosophy, in the fifth century B.C., when he had considered that learning was a lifelong process for the human being.

Ladies and Gentlemen,

Education is one of the fields of competence of UNESCO and occupies a prominent position within the Organisation's programme and the Executive Council's reflections and discussions at all sessions. UNESCO has been continuously striving to ensure that everyone benefit from education everywhere in the world. It is pursuing its efforts in accordance with its mission and in cooperation with the member states with a view to securing education for all on a lifelong basis, and ensuring its quality, reforming and modernising the educational systems, in an effort to fight poverty, social exclusion and violence, improve the living conditions of all populations and instil the values of human rights, peace, sustainable development, justice and tolerance among people worldwide. The prominent role of the Organisation in this field was reiterated at international level at the 2000 Dakar Forum on Education. The international community has committed itself to work hard to ensure that the goal of Education

For All with its six basic principles become effective by 2015. These principles are the following: ensure access for all children of school age to education free of charge and of acceptable quality; eliminate gender inequality in education; bring down illiteracy rates by half among adults; promote the concern for education in early childhood to a large extent; increase education opportunities among young and adult populations and improve every aspect of quality in education.

While basic education seeks to meet the common needs of all people, secondary education is requested to disclose and encourage gifts and talents in their diversity. The secondary education phase is a very critical phase in the life of a student for he/she starts to look at the world and life with curiosity, interest and concern. At this stage, personality becomes crystallised and seeks its way to the future. Therefore education plays the role of indicating that the road is not closed, but rather open to science whatever the circumstances, and that several opportunities are lying ahead. In this phase, students begin to use their minds and resort to the necessary standards of conscience that allow them to respect and preserve their authenticity and, at the same time, engage in the process of modernity. Preserving authenticity also means respecting diversity and difference so as to live together in harmony and concord in a better society and in a better world in which opportunities are offered to all, without poverty, oppression or discrimination.

Attention should also be placed on school books and curricula. School books and curricula should be free from any deceptive values that encourage hatred or ignorance of others. What is needed is that school books should carry the seeds of openness towards and knowledge of the others. The more we get to know the others, the deeper will be our love to them; likewise, the more the others get to know us, the deeper will be their love to us. Human beings are enemies of what they don't know.

The Sultanate of Oman is striving to build a broad vision in order to carry out an educational reform based on the principles of commitment, inclusiveness, complementary, justice while catching up with technological development. I am confident that these efforts will, God willing, be crowned with success and that the Sultanate will know how to address the challenges facing our world and will move ahead to achieve further progress and development.

I cannot help expressing my pain and affliction at the practices of torture and killing to which the children of Palestine are exposed in total opposition with the principles of peace and common moral values, as well as the acts of destruction and damage that have struck the cultural heritage and administrative and educational institutions in the Palestinian territories, and the absurd act of depriving them of their legitimate right to school, education, health care and a decent living in a safe, stable and peaceful world. We should also remember the children of Afghanistan and Iraq and all children deprived of these basic legitimate rights wherever they are.

Ladies and Gentlemen,

UNESCO has several tasks and programmes, but a single mission which consists in building the human mind, in other words building human conscience to prevent dangers and establish a sustainable peace. Our organisation was born from a wonderful idea which goes like this: "as wars were born in the human mind, the bulwark of peace should be erected in the human mind", and which was pronounced by the American poet, Archibald McLeash, one of UNESCO's founding fathers. This idea was then inserted in the constitutive charter of the organisation. We cannot say that this mission is now outdated, for the events taking place in our world today remind us that this mission is still young, up-to-date and necessary. Our task is to work and find the best ways and means for implementing it everywhere on earth.

In conclusion, I would like to reiterate my thanks to His Excellency Yahya bin Saud Al- Sulaimi and to the Omani authorities for the generous hospitality which has been reserved to us and for the excellent conditions made to ensure the full success of this conference. I also extend my fraternal salutations to Dr. Fawzia bint Nasser Al- Farsi, Secretary General of the Ministry of Education and thank her for her effective and distinct contribution within the Executive Council of UNESCO. I also wish to express my warmest greetings to my colleague and brother Dr. Moussa bin Hasan bin Jaafar, the Ambassador and Permanent Delegate of Oman to UNESCO for the active and dynamic role he plays in the life of the Organisation and for lifting high the banner of his country within this important international forum.

Thank you for your attention.

6. *A speech presented by a representative from the Islamic Organisation for Education, Science and Culture (ISESCO)*

Praise be to Allah, Peace be upon the Prophet Muhammad, upon his kin and kith

Your Highnesses and Excellencies,
Your Excellency Director General of UNESCO,
Excellencies,
Honourable participants,
Assalamu alaikum warahmatullah wabarakatuh,

It is my pleasure to convey to you all, at the beginning of this address, the salutations of Dr. Abdulaziz bin Othman Al-Tuwaijri, the Director General of the Islamic Organisation for Education, Science and Culture (ISESCO), and to extend to you his best wishes of success for this international conference.

I am also very pleased to express my warmest thanks to His Excellency Yahya bin Saud bin Mansoor Al-Sulaimi, Minister of Education in the Sultanate of Oman for the kind invitation addressed to the Islamic Organisation for Education, Science and Culture to attend this International Conference whose works have, with the grace of Allah, been crowned with success.

Education issues and namely secondary education issues which this International Conference was conveyed to address some of its most important aspects are closely related to the question of development in its broad sense and whose purpose is to educate the human being—who is the pillar of the welfare of nations and civilisations—to use all potential resources and invest all possible capabilities with the view to bringing about profound civilisational change that is in accordance with the nature of the local cultural identity and at the same time that meets the spirit of modern times.

The extraordinary scientific and information revolution and cultural development have become self-evident and it is no longer possible for education systems and philosophy or school curricula and programs to ignore these ongoing technological mutations which are taking place in the world.

ISESCO is fully aware that the Islamic world is today confronting numerous interlaced challenges in different domains among which is the field of education. Such challenges are related to the modernisation and reform and education and to the need for linking education with a training approach capable of coping with the technical and professional developments in a manner that helps to curb unemployment.

Your Highnesses and Excellencies,
Honourable participants,

The issues addressed by this Conference are at the heart of the objectives laid down in every plan of action of ISESCO. Education has always held an important place within ISESCO's programs, be it in terms of the extent of these programs, or the budget allocated for their implementation or the projects and works achieved within the framework of a coherent approach which takes its inspiration, in its essence and profoundness, from the educational philosophy in Islamic civilisation which is firmly premised on the teachings of the Islamic religion.

In conclusion, I would like to praise the high quality of the working papers presented at this important International Conference as well as the recommendations issued from its working sessions. It was indeed a successful conference by all standards and at all levels.

May Allah assist you and guide your steps. Thank you for your attention.

Wassalamu alaikum warahmatullah wabarakatuh.

Final Report of the Third Meeting of the Interagency Consultative Group on Secondary Education Reform and Youth Affairs, Third Meeting, Paris, 26-28 March 2002. © UNESCO. Courtesy: UNESCO.

Part-2

SECONDARY EDUCATION REFORM AND YOUTH AFFAIRS

Final Report of the Third Meeting of the Interagency Consultative Group on Secondary Education Reforms and Youth Affairs, Third Meeting, Paris, 26-28 March 2002. © UNESCO. Courtesy: UNESCO.

6

Introduction and Background

Set up in 1999, the Consultative Group provides a forum for inter-agency consultation. Its Original objectives were:

- to exchange information and ideas;
- to share on-going work that optimises reform efforts;
- to identify areas of potential synergy and collaboration.

Following the two previous meetings of the Group in 1999 and 2000, two principles were proposed:

- to base its future work on 'The Dakar Framework for Action';
- to concentrate on a limited number of priority themes within that Framework.

This third meeting was attended by over fifty representatives from international organisations, bilateral agencies, non-governmental organisations and various UNESCO offices and Institutes, as well as by two international observers (see Annex 2).

The meeting's specific objectives were:

- to review developments since the February 2000 Meeting, especially regarding major work undertaken, new research results and policy orientations;

- to identify the main implications of the Dakar Framework for our own work at secondary level and for selected important themes;
- to identify possible areas for collaboration over the next two years;
- to agree on the Group's future role, functions and working modalities over the next two years.

Accordingly, the agenda (see Annex 1) fell into three main parts. The plenary sessions on the first day reviewed progress since the last meeting. On the second day, work took place in Thematic Groups to consider the four themes that had been introduced at the end of the first day. Finally, the Consultative Group met in plenary session on day three to consider reports from the Thematic Groups and agree ways forward.

7

Opening Session

The first session of the first day was chaired by Sir John Daniel, ADG/ED, UNESCO, who opened the third meeting with a Welcome Address. In it he stressed the importance of secondary education, highlighting its central position in relation to primary education, youth affairs and higher education. He linked it directly to the Dakar Framework, especially Goal 3:

> *'ensuring that the learning needs of all young people and adults are met through equitable access to appropriate learning and life-skills programmes'*

UNESCO was responding directly to requests form member states seeking guidance on how best to achieve this and other Dakar goals. One key question concerned the nature and scope of Basic Education. Another was that the present emphasis on primary education was inevitably increasing the demand for secondary education and posing issues of access. A third, and related issue, concerned gender equity in secondary education, specifically mentioned in Goal 5 of the Dakar Framework. This Consultative Group offered a good opportunity for networking and exchange of ideas about emerging trends and ways of providing help to Member States on these and related matters.

Mr Wataru Iwamoto, Director of the Division of Secondary, Technical and Vocational Education, UNESCO, chaired the next short session in which the provisional agenda was adopted. Ms Sonia Bahri, Chief of the Section for General Secondary Education, provided an introduction and overview of the meeting.

8

Progress Reports

In advance of the meeting, Group members had been requested to prepare short progress reports/summaries of activities in the field of secondary education reform and youth affairs since the last meeting in 2000, under the following headings:

(a) the main strategies adopted;

(b) ranked priorities amongst four themes:

- Needs of Adolescents at secondary level;
- Reforming the Curriculum-Content, Examinations and Accreditation;
- Linking Secondary Education and TVE;
- The Roles of Teachers, Principals and other School Personnel.

(c) major work/actions;

(d) the main regions/countries focused on;

(e) major partners;

(f) website information.

Members welcomed this method of summarising progress and twenty such reports were received. All are posted on the GINIE web site (www.ginie.org) and on the Consultative Group site (www.seryp.org/paris).

Accordingly, what follows simply highlights some of the main points made in the brief presentations, in the order in which they were made during the plenary session.

- Mr Ratteree mentioned the strategic priority being given by the ***ILO*** to lifelong learning, teaching personnel and human resource development.
- Mr Brown ***(UNHCR)*** emphasised that only 3% of refugee children go to secondary school and that refugee education falls between normal funding budgets.
- Mr Guerrero reported that ***UNICEF*** would publish a position paper on secondary education and a joint report with ***UNFPA*** and WHO on *'Meeting the Development and Participation Rights of Adolescent Girls'* in the coming year.
- Mr Linden said that the ***World Bank*** had pursued two themes since the last meeting: supporting the implementation of sector-wide programmes; analysing issues in post-basic education in a lifelong learning perspective. Case studies of secondary education were posted on the website.
- Mr. Teisseire said that, having adopted the six Dakar goals, the ***AIF*** was concentrating on three strategic areas—the French language, basic education and technical and vocational training.
- Mr Wimberley stated that, having completed its project on secondary education reforms the ***Council of Europe*** was concentrating curriculum-oriented projects on education for democratic citizenship, language learning and history.
- Mr McKenzie reported that the ***OECD's*** new mandate was organised around the theme *'Investing in Competencies for All'*, incorporating a range of current and planned activities in secondary education.

- Ms Phillips indicated that, within its mandate for promoting open learning in 54 Commonwealth countries, ***COL*** was engaged in a wide range of secondary education initiatives. These included developing materials for English, mathematics, science and technology, as well as professional development for chief education officers.
- The observer from the ***Sultanate of Oman,*** Mr Mohammed Salim Al Yakoubi, informed the meeting about the planned international conference on secondary education, to be held in Oman during December 2002.
- Mme Fouilhoux said that, post Dakar and under the broad theme of 'Changes in the Teaching Profession', ***EI*** was focusing on three projects - technical and vocational training, new partnerships and globalisation.
- Mr Vedeler stated that, in budgetary terms, secondary education was currently a limited priority for ***NORAD*** but that its emphasis would shift to secondary education via bilateral projects with individual countries on life skills and girls education.
- Mr McClusky described the three main strategies currently adopted by ***USAID*** as workforce development, school to work and support systems for 'out-of-school' unemployed children and youth, with a particular emphasis on fundamental life-skills.
- Ms Drennen stated that the ***IBO*** was introducing three pilot initiatives—in trans-disciplinary subjects, distance teaching and new languages of instruction.
- Mr Loing said that the ***ICDE*** was working mainly at university level on access and quality assurance. In secondary education its focus was on trans-national assessment.

- Ms Sauvage told the meeting that, at its recent general conference, ***IFUW*** had adopted an action plan directed towards the educational opportunities of adolescent girls, including adolescent mothers, children in armed conflict situations and child soldiers in post-conflict situations.
- Mr Boukary summarised the work of ***ADEA*** as a forum and a network for the development of education in Africa. It influences secondary education indirectly, for example, via working groups on educational financing and on the teaching profession in sub-Saharan African countries.
- Mr Boyer said that the ***Commission nationale française pour l'UNESCO*** saw secondary education as pivotal within the context of the Delors Commission on Lifelong Learning and was working on projects on the Role of Teachers with the Council of Europe.
- Ms Gear summarised the work of the **British *Council*** in 112 countries, highlighting its 'Connecting Futures' initiative for young people aged 25-24, its 'Citizenship Education and Human Rights Education' projects and its Teacher International Professional Development Programme'.
- Ms Anselme stated that the ***RET*** had several programmes relevant to secondary education including those on support for local schools receiving refugees, on support for education in refugee camps, on teacher training and direct support via materials and equipment.
- Ms Bahri overviewed ***UNESCO's*** work and strategy on secondary education in all countries of the world. Post Dakar, it was seeking to enhance access and improve relevance,

effectiveness and equity via international policy dialogue and assistance, with particular reference to specified key issues including gender, marginalised groups, renewal of curriculum and methods, the new role of teachers and education professionals, technical and vocational education, life skills and counselling programmes. Major action at international level since the last meeting included the *'International Expert Meeting on General Secondary Education in the Twenty-first Century'* held in Beijing, China in May 2001.

- Ms Braslavsky summarised IBE's strategies as concentrating on the gathering and dissemination of information and good practice related to curriculum reform in secondary and youth education. Methods included the last edition of World Data on Education and the 46th UNESCO International Conference on Education.
- Ms Caillods said that ***IIEP*** was conducting research on financing the expansion of secondary education and for enhancing equity of access. A major book had just been published.
- Mr MacLean reported that, in order to support the reform of secondary education and help prepare youth for changes resulting from globalisation, ***UNEVOC's*** strategies included the provision of a clearing house on best practice and human resource development for key personnel at country level.
- Mr Zhou Nanzhao, ***Bangkok office,*** spoke of UNESCO's objectives for the Asia-Pacific Region as including further expansion of equal access, diversifying institutional structures and improved teacher education via a Regional Forum, a high school principals' training programme innovation dissemination strategies.
- Mr Billeh, ***Beirut office,*** said that Ministries in the Arab States were placing an increasing emphasis on

the reform of secondary education. Emerging issues included the distinction between basic and secondary education and the diversification of the latter's provision, for instance in the form of vocational education at work and via other agencies.

- Mr Mariro reported that the ***Dakar Office,*** together with the World Bank, had organised the *'Regional Workshop on Secondary Education Renewal in Africa'* in Mauritius, in December 2001. It was also carrying out various studies on the post-Dakar situation, for example on human resource strategy and the teaching profession, basic education, and transition to secondary education.
- Ms Macedo said the Santiago office was carrying out a study on regional reform and promoting a network on exchange between Ministries.
- Mr Chinapah from the ***Division for the Promotion of Quality in Education*** made a brief presentation on the Division's work on indicators, learning outcomes and minimum learning competencies as a means of promoting the capacity building of nations.
- Ms Henriques-Mueller said the work of the ***Youth Co-ordination Unit, Bureau of Strategic Planning*** was shifting its emphasis to the demand side. She highlighted three achievements since 2000—contacting and supporting student organisations throughout the world, strengthening non-formal education networks, and inviting scholars to spend sabbaticals at UNESCO aiming at the development of curriculum reform.
- Mr Radi said the ***Division of Basic Education*** was focused on the balance of the education system overall. Post Dakar, basic education was not the sole objective. Secondary education was increasingly important as a means of providing access to higher education.

- In a written contribution, Mr Kinelev (not present) referred to the work *IITE* is undertaking in supporting the enhancement of national capacities for the application of information and communication technology (ICT) via, for example, applied research projects, expert meetings and analytic surveys.

- In the final contribution to this session, Ms McClure updated the meeting on the progress of the web-site produced in collaboration between UNESCO, USAID and the University of Pittsburgh. She did so by presenting the site visually on the screen, pointing out that this conference's own site (www.seryp.org/paris) is part of a wider information network site (www.ginie.org).

9

Round Table Presentations and Discussion

After lunch on Day 1, there were short presentations and discussion on several major topics. The six papers for these presentations are available on the conference web site so only selected points are mentioned here.

The first two papers were on the broad topic, *Secondary education reform and expansion in the light of Education for All (EFA) and the Dakar framework for Action*. Paper 1, by Mr Singh, was presented in his absence by Mr Mputu. It discussed the ways in which concepts of basic, primary and secondary education are actually operationalised in Member States and presented data on enrolment and transition rates. Challenges highlighted included the limited opportunities for progression from the primary to secondary stages, factors in primary education that are hindering developments at secondary level and the impact of tertiary education and the labour market. A complementary paper, by Ms Cavicchioni, was entitled *'The Challenge of Achieving Gender Parity in Basic Education'*. It argued that, although disparities had decreased from 1990 to 1998 in most countries, they continued in some countries (e.g. in Central and Western Africa). Moreover, they are more pronounced at the secondary stage, increasingly favouring girls in more advanced systems.

The third paper dealt with the second broad topic, *'Financing Secondary Education in Developing Countries:*

strategies for sustainable development' was presented by Ms Caillods and was extracted from her recent book with Keith Lewin. In it, she revisited and commented on the rationale for investment at secondary level, analysed data on the financial challenge to policy development in secondary education, summarised country case studies and outlined policy options for sustainable growth.

The next three papers were on the broad topic *'Diversifying delivery: distance education and other alternative delivery systems'*. Paper 4 was presented by Mr Linden who offered two initial propositions: that the present methods of delivery were too expensive and that the present methods of secondary education in OECD countries had failed when judged by the criterion of their high rates of functional illiteracy. Accordingly we should look to models like double shift schools, night schools, study centres and non-formal rural education as cost-effective alternatives. In so doing, account must be taken of key issues like accreditation, quality materials and cost structures. In paper 5, Mr Loing argued that ICT priority issues - and thus possible ways forward - vary across countries. Access is the priority in the least developed countries (LDCs) and digital radio is an example of a solution in Africa. Integration into pedagogy (i.e. *'webagogy'*) is the main issue in developed countries—the Australian virtual schooling service offers a way forward there. Harmonisation is a priority in European countries where the 'Schoolnet' project is a promising innovation. In paper 6, Ms Phillips argued that a major challenge was to provide more opportunities for secondary school level education which are of high quality, relevant to the learners and both accessible and affordable. Conventional schooling is too expensive and time-consuming and is often either not accessible or prohibitively expensive. Open Schooling offers an alternative which, to be effective, must be timely in its implementation, deliver quality education to a large number of learners, be economical and cost-effective and not require a large number of trained teachers.

Issues raised in discussion included the following:

- many basic education level teachers have only been educated to secondary level, so secondary education also fulfils an important function in this respect;
- gross enrolment figures for secondary education are important but, because they include many over-age students, they over-estimate participation rates for the secondary age cohorts;
- teachers in secondary education face a wide range of student age and maturity, with significant implications for quality;
- because there are many factors affecting girls' access to education, more disaggregated data are needed as well as data on quality;
- there is evidence about the negative impact of poor health on student learning, especially at primary level, but more studies are needed;
- more studies are also needed on the unintended impact of various financial incentive schemes on access and retention. For instance, in one case when girls were given exemption from fees, some head-teachers said they would no longer take girls because they did not receive the fees;
- several members questioned the desirability of designing secondary education primarily for university entrance;
- policy makers were urged to be cautious when considering increased finance for higher education. They should also focus on reducing inefficiencies.

10

Round Table Themes

Four themes were identified as possible priority areas for future work:

1. 'Meeting the needs of adolescents at secondary level'
2. 'Reforming the curriculum: content, examinations and accreditation'
3. 'Linking secondary education and technical and vocational education (TVE)'
4. 'The changing roles of teachers, principals and other school personnel'

In the meeting itself, the authors of the two lead papers for each theme briefly introduced them in the final plenary session of day 1. They were then presented at greater length to the members of the Thematic Groups who met throughout Day 2 to discuss and analyse the papers in detail, using a framework of common questions. Rapporteurs for each Group presented preliminary accounts of these discussions to the last plenary session on Day 2. Final summaries were then produced overnight and presented and discussed in the first plenary session of Day 3. All eight papers are posted on the conference web site so, once again, only highlights are mentioned here in the context of summaries of the working group and plenary discussions.

Thematic Group 1: Meeting the Needs of Adolescents

Mr Guerrero's lead paper (*'Education for Adolescents'*) saw adolescence as a unique opportunity to break the vicious circle of poverty, gender discrimination, violence and poor health and nutrition. As one example, UNICEF's focus on girls sought to enhance life skills, catch up/second chance, quality education and participation. Mr Zhou's lead paper (*'Meeting the Needs of Adolescents'*) stated that over 50% of the world's population are under the age 25 and 20% are adolescents (10-19 years old). Youth was defined as the age range 15-24 and hence secondary education covered most adolescent and youth years. The paper summarised the diverse needs of adolescents and proposed five strategies for meeting them: multi-sectoral cooperation, participatory approaches, inter-agency coordination, integrated programmes and partnerships/networking.

Ms Gear, the Rapporteur, summarised the day's discussion as follows.

1. What are the Main Issues Raised by the Lead Papers?

- Adolescence brings with it very special needs – this is a transitional phase from childhood to adulthood;
- Because of different contexts/structures in educational provision we cannot fit this age range into a traditional 'box' in terms of education level i.e. primary/secondary. We therefore need policies to ensure at each educational level these special needs are recognised. Diverse needs include gender discrimination, work situations, learning in conflict, etc;
- To meet these special needs a learner-centred approach, which addresses issues of relevance and quality, is particularly important.

2. Who is Doing What?

Each member of the group will provide examples of any work their agency is involved with in this area to be included on the GINIE website.

3. *What Else Needs to be Done*

- Development of youth-friendly indicators within the EFA goals—particularly relating to quality. This is to ensure that adolescents themselves are finding their education of quality and of relevance.
- We need to find out what system of delivery of education for this age group meets adolescents' needs in different contexts, and ensure agencies work to their comparative advantage.
- Accreditation is a key drive for young people. An example was given of working with young people in refugee camps—where this issue was particularly important to these young people thinking ahead to their future.

5. *How, Where and What Can Partners Work on Together?*

The group agreed that a priority was delivery systems for meeting the needs of adolescents at different levels i.e. basic skills, work/life competencies, post basic, etc.

6. *What are the Thematic Group's Main Conclusions*

- A focus on this age-range or life-cycle period, i.e. ADOLESCENCE, can provide a useful 'lens' through which to look at programmes of delivery of basic education and post-basic education (life/ work skills/competencies) i.e. not to be 'stuck' within the concept of age but outcomes i.e. basic level/skills and the secondary level competencies leading to work and/or higher education (these can occur at different ages).
- To ensure that the specific needs of adolescents are met at all levels. The policy implications are that all teachers and trainers need training in meeting the needs of adolescents.
- This relates to a number of the goals of the Dakar Framework for Action because of the reference to

quality of basic education/life-long learning/ relevance.

- Education should be relevant to the specific learner i.e. focussing on this age range/period of life again emphasises the importance of the shift between supplyside to demand-side of education to inform the policy process.

Thematic Group 2: Reforming the Curriculum: Content, Examinations and Accreditation

Ms Braslavsky's lead paper compared and contrasted traditional and current notions of curriculum reform. In the 21st century, policy makers believe that what, when and how to learn has to be defined and re-defined at different levels and moments and that a contract between all protagonists is necessary. She posed a range of questions and indicated that the IBE was responding by analysing trends, capacity building, policy dialogue (e.g. the 46th ICE) and evaluation of curriculum products. Ms Drennen's lead paper dealt with the IBO's approach to content (e.g. promoting coherence and continuity from 3-19 years), examinations (e.g. promoting teacher assessment) and accreditation (e.g. promoting exchange of ideas/reforms between national systems). She illustrated these ideas in relation to three programmes - primary, middle and diploma.

Ms Sauvage, the Rapporteur, summarised the day's discussion as follows:

1. What are the Main Issues Raised by the Lead Papers?

The documents that were presented to us relate very interesting experiences but do not reply to the question: how to reform the curriculum? We thus started the discussion with the necessity of defining secondary education and its objectives:

- to adopt a student-centred approach rather than a discipline—or a structure-centered approach;
- to help in the emergence of competences;

- to structure the mind;
- to help the student to locate/situate himself in an environment, and gain control of his environment;
- to help the student find his own way and how he wishes to enter adult life.

Curriculum should be thought of as a process and not as a product. It is a kind of contract between learners and institutions, between society and institutions. This process must take into account the increasing autonomy of the students during the secondary education level.

Curriculum content should seek a balance between:

- a global method and traditional disciplines;
- general education and vocational education;
- a global context and a local context;

and should give an important role to personal development (e.g. critical eye, analytical method) and to the knowledge of cultural diversity.

But a reform should not be a "hollow victory". It should be based on experiences between countries that can be compared, on international experiences, and should envisage a transfer of patterns in the direction South-North, as well as in the direction North-South.

A reform can be envisaged from different viewpoints: teacher training, structure of classes, school textbooks. It should always take into consideration the economic aspect, the gender balance, the health of partners, etc. Little time has been devoted to the accreditation that the Group preferred to call "quality assurance". The problem remains the same when one comes to speak of training flexibility. That was the case during the discussion, in particular when it concerned groups in difficulty such as young refugees issued from armed conflicts, and girls.

Globalisation in this matter can be detrimental to young people as a comparative evaluation would put them in a disadvantaged position when it comes to the world of work.

4. ***Who is Doing What About These Issues at Secondary Level in the Post-Dakar Context?***

One of the goals of the Dakar Framework for Action is "Ensuring that the learning needs of all young people and adults are met through equitable access to appropriate learning and life skills' programmes". This goal includes necessarily what we call secondary education. Yet it has been proven that secondary education is the missing link of the Education for All (EFA) agenda. All countries need to enlarge the possibilities of this level of education, including developed countries. As regards girls, it seemed to us essential that a renewed curriculum should be one of their main concerns towards girls as well as towards boys. It would also be necessary that these reforms go along with a specific training aimed at teachers as well as at parents in the field of stereotypes which are often at the basis of the refusal of girls to study scientific subjects. As regards groups in difficulty (in crisis), it appeared to us that flexibility is an essential component to help the young people belonging to these groups.

5. ***How, Where and on What Can Partners Work Together?***

The International Bureau of Education (IBE) proposed (i) that this Interagency Consultative Group work jointly for the preparation of the 47th session of the International Conference on Education (ICE) which will focus on many aspects of secondary education, and (ii) to enhance the exchange of ideas and experiences through the setting up of electronic forums on curriculum reform at secondary level.

6. ***What are the Thematic Group's Main Conclusions?***

If there is a certain consensus on the objectives of primary education and its quantifiable outcomes, there is no consensus as regards secondary education. A new vision is necessary before any reform takes place. In view of this reform, the support of teachers is needed as well as that of civil society. One has to be innovative in this field and more creative than ever.

Thematic Group 3: Secondary Education for the World of Work and Technical and Vocational Education and Training

Mr McKenzie's lead paper (*'Linking general and vocational learning in secondary education'*) drew upon a recent comparative review of education-to-work transition in 14 OECD countries. He argued that vocational learning need to be strengthened for several reasons including to make school learning more interesting and to improve the transition to both further education and work. He identified several reform trends (e.g. increasing student choice, more flexible pathways) and characterised effective education-to-work transition systems as having several features including workplace experience, 'youth friendly' labour markets and tight safety nets. Mr McClusky's lead paper (*'Workforce development impacts in secondary education'*) said that, rather than starting with education reform, USAID had analysed labour markets in order to develop better workforce skills-development systems. Amongst the cited consequences of this approach were the emergence of certification standards, curriculum adjustments to meet labour market needs, experiential learning, emphasis on entrepreneurship, private/public partnerships and more responsive higher education institutions.

Mr Maclean, the Rapporteur, summarised the day's discussion as follows.

*1. **What are the Main Issues Raised by the Lead Papers?***

- *Changing definition of vocational education*

There is need to adopt a broader concept of vocational education and for it to be considered as part of lifelong learning. The definition of vocational education needs to ensure that it is seen as an alternative and equal form of education which is valid just as much as academic education. Vocational and educational programmes are generally preparation for work or for a particular occupation while general education is more a preparation for life.

- *Place in the curriculum*

Vocational education is not a single generic way of educating but can appear in different ways in the curriculum. For example traditional courses such as metal work; working in a team to solve a problem when it comes to learning by doing; and, drawing examples in a range of subjects (such as mathematics) which relate to actual situations outside the school.

- *Importance of cross-cutting themes*

There is no single model regarding what secondary education and vocational education should look like since this depends on the particular context of education system. There are a number of critical cross-cutting themes which impact on the relationship between vocational education and secondary education. For example: gender; financial cost; rural urban location; level of technology; poverty; entrepreneurship; how to accommodate marginalised groups; teachers; availability of resources; governance/ policy and planning; It is also important to stress *vocational learning* rather than just the notion of vocational *education*.

- *Flexibility and alternative pathways*

The aim should be to construct pathways that are broad and long in order that learners can keep their options open. There is also a need to ensure that groups like university gatekeepers accept that vocational education can be cognitively complex and should be valued; and success in vocational programmes should enable transfer into academic streams.

It is important to ensure that all doors remain open for competent learners for as long as possible in the learning cycle through maximizing flexibility and transfer between vocational education and academic education. This involves increasing the status of vocational education and breaking stereotypes that still persist in certain places: for instance, where simplistic distinctions between blue collar (vocational education) and white collar (academic education) work exist and where vocational education is regarded as working with one's hand while academic education is working with one's head. These distinctions are often no longer valid.

In addition, given the rate of economic and social change, people will change their work many times over their life and so preparation should not be too specific to a particular occupation. The concept of lifelong learning and career-long professional development become issues of importance. There is a need for a more generic preparation with a focus on basic skills which maximize flexibility and promote the ability to prepare for a global employment market. The development of qualifications frameworks that enables the transferability of qualifications between countries.

2. Who is Doing What About These Issues at Secondary Level in the Post-Dakar Context?

OECD is undertaking follow up to the report issued in 2000 on "from initial education to working life". Fifteen countries have agreed to pool their resources to focus greater attention on guidance and counselling on a lifelong learning context. This is important to enable young people to know the options open to them. The study, which is to be undertaken in collaboration with the World Bank, will be concluded at the end of year 2002. OECD is also undertaking a study on lifelong learning and the role of qualifications in facilitating a move between sectors. As part of this, they are examining what countries are doing to recognise non-formal learning. In addition OECD has just launched a study on the teaching profession which examines what societies are demanding of schools including a broader notion of vocational education. In the next stage of PISA, longitudinal studies of young people moving through the education system into vocational education, higher education, etc., will be undertaken.

In ***Norway,*** the Ministry of Education has examined the matter of providing a diversified and streamlined system of vocational education. Attempts have also been made to provide greater flexibility in what was previously a more uniform system. ***NORAD*** are undertaking activities which seek to make aid-assistance more focused both in terms of content and with regard to particular countries. A relatively small percentage of the total budget currently goes to vocational education but there are attempts to increase the allocation of funds to this sector. A matter being currently debated concerns what the priority education programmes should be in the future with many feeling that as EFA proves successful, much greater emphasis should be placed on secondary education and TVET. Meeting the needs of girls, adults and lifelong learning and teacher-training are all key considerations.

In ***USAID,*** there is a move to examine broader educational considerations rather than just EFA. However, the programmes being developed are conceptualised as part of the Dakar follow-up. The reform of secondary education is seen as a very important part of the process of workforce development. There is a need to improve the competitive edge when it comes to employment through, for example, focusing on the types of linkages between education and the private sector. In many countries, a greater emphasis needs to be placed on meeting the needs of youth with particular reference to improving the link between education and the world of work.

The ***World Bank*** considers secondary education as part of lifelong learning and not in isolation. The WB is going to hold a meeting on lifelong learning in developing countries in Stuttgart, in Autumn 2002. An area of particular emphasis is "knowledge for development" regarding education and training. The WB has more than 20 country-based projects in all regions on secondary education and TVET. They have also published a number of case studies on secondary education and TVET in several countries, e.g. Brazil. They are also closely involved with the PISA work in order to help improve the reliability and richness of data available to policy makers when it comes to making decisions. In Africa, the WB is conducting studies on secondary education and vocational education and training with particular reference to informal sector-training, financing of VET, etc. Matters regarding the vocationalisation and enterprise education are being undertaken in collaboration with OECD and IIEP.

At ***Headquarters*** level, UNESCO is working in the area of guidance and counseling for employment and a book will be published on issues in this area in the future. A part of the study is being undertaken in both English- and French-speaking Africa to develop training modules relating to the development of guidance programmes. The stress is on girls and women. A Guidance Center is being established in Malawi. Pilot activities are being undertaken to improve access and equity with regard to girls in TVET; and follow-up is occurring regarding the revised recommendations on TVET, passed by the Member States at the last General Conference.

In the ***UNESCO-UNEVOC*** Centre in Bonn, the emphasis with regard to secondary education and TVET has been on: interagency collaboration regarding programmes at the secondary level for vocational education (Voc. Ed.); strengthening and upgrading of the UNEVOC network which consists of 205 centres in 136 countries; the development of relevant programme activities in Southern Africa, West Africa, Middle East, Asia, Pacific and Central Asian Republics. With regard to knowledge management, the Bonn Centre has an extensive publications programme involving an international handbook on vocational education as well as a book series on the same area. A knowledge-management website on TVET is being established with assistance from SAP.

UNESCO Beirut has initiated a policy dialogue with the Arab States regarding secondary education and vocational education. They are also providing technical backstopping assistance to Member States regarding TVET as part of the promotion of national capacity building. Networking in the region to bring together partner institutions involved with vocational education has been promoted and currently a meeting is being planned to facilitate the identification of areas of common interest between countries with regard to secondary education and vocational education. Outside funding to be sought for projects in the areas so identified.

3. What Else Needs to be Done at Secondary Level in the Post-Dakar Context?

- Greater emphasis on promoting flexibility in TVET and academic education programmes
- Greater ease of transferability between vocational and academic streams
- Improved status of vocational education as a valued form of education
- Greater stress on meeting the needs of vulnerable groups such as women and girls, those in poverty, ethnic and racial minority groups, etc.
- Need to develop greater partnerships with regard to TVET, programme delivery and assessment including involvement of private enterprises

4. How, Where and on What Partners Work Together?

- General agreement between the partner agencies that they can work together to address the range of issues presented in part 1. above
- Areas of particular emphasis are: improved access to vocational education; strengthening enough grading; quality assurance; equity issues with particular reference to the education of girls and women, etc.
- See areas of interest of different agencies as referred to under 2. above.
- As a follow-up to this meeting, agencies who participated in thematic group 3 to explore areas for joint activities.

5. *What are the Thematic Group's Main Conclusion?*

- There is a need to adopt a broader concept of vocational education as part of lifelong learning.
- Vocational education is not a single way of educating people since many possible half-ways can occur
- More needs to be done to examine the impact of key cross-cutting themes (eg Gender; poverty; teachers; etc. with regard to impact on vocational and secondary education)
- Greater effort needs to be taken to construct pathways which enable people to keep their learning options open as long as possible
- Greater flexibility needs to occur between vocational and academic education including the mutual recognition of qualifications
- Private enterprises have an important role to play with regarding to the framing, delivery and assessment of vocational programmes
- There are many areas of common concern between partners such as OECD, USAID, UNESCO, etc. with regard to secondary education and vocational education. As a result closer collaboration and cooperation is certainly possible between these various agencies.

Thematic Group 4: The Changing Roles of Teachers, School Leaders and Other Education Personnel (OEP)

Ms Fouilloux's's lead paper *('The situation of second level teachers and educational staff)* argued that the education professions were having to change as a result of pressures form several sources - economic, social, knowledge shifts, new technologies and productivity. Yet there were certain essential factors in the roles of teachers - as designers of content and learning, as participants in the management of the system and as team-workers with other specialist staff.

(e.g. educational psychologists). All these pressures and factors had implications for teacher recruitment, training, working conditions, payment and status. Given the increasing feminisation of the teaching profession in some countries of the world and the low proportion in some others, the implications for women had special significance. Mr Bolam's lead paper (*'Changing roles and training needs of principals'*) summarised selected research and experience in order to demonstrate that secondary school principals are critically important to school improvement and that their roles are changing substantially. It then considered ways in which illustrative national training and development strategies have been modified in response to these changes and suggested a framework for possible future collaborative work.

Ms McClure, the Rapporteur, summarised the day's discussion as follows:

1. What are the Main Issues Raised by the Lead Papers?

The group focused on *'what drives changing roles?'* and concluded that the following issues were important:

- changing economic environments—economic conditions putting pressure on families and schools to help ensure the economic success of all children (smaller families, greater market economic identity;
- changing social environment—conditions put pressure on schools and communities to address issues of adolescent development (reproductive health, HIV/AIDS, political and social identity);
- changing understandings of the roles of teachers, school leaders and other education personnel:
  - ❐ education as institutional competition—markets and consumer choices;
  - ❐ education as participatory planning—increased roles of community; stakeholders—accountability and transparency;

- ❒ education as professional design—teachers as sources of innovation;
- ❒ creators of materials, methods and curriculum

There was a need:

- for more comprehensive profiles of teachers, school leaders, and other education personnel not principally involved in either teaching or school leadership (eg school inspectors, librarians, counselors, etc.);
- to fill gaps to better inform EFA action plans – special emphasis needed on school leaders – also need to broaden perceptions of who works in schools, including former teachers who have moved on;
- for clearer understanding of what training is needed to meet changing roles at all levels–costs and certification–new types of delivery systems;
- for better articulation between training for general and vocational education;
- for innovation in new education roles (e.g. mentors, near peer tutors).

2. *Who is Doing what About these Issues at Secondary Level in the Post-Dakar Context?*

Several group members were doing work on these and related topics as indicated in their summaries for the meeting (see conference website) and item 4, below.

3. *What are the Gaps that Need to be Filled?*

- Need for better quality indicators related to issues of changing roles eg:
  - ❒ numbers of teachers, school leaders and OEP at national and sub-national levels;
  - ❒ profile data related to age, gender (feminisation of profession);

- ❐ qualifications;
- ❐ salaries and benefits (health care, pensions, etc.);
- ❐ class size;
- ❐ pupil/teacher ratio;
- ❐ workload;
- ❐ quality outcomes beyond national exams.

- In urban/rural schools, there was a need to better understand:
  - ❐ best practices for effective teaching and learning;
  - ❐ bridges to the community;
  - ❐ centres for innovation;
  - ❐ possibilities for collaboration.
- In crisis situations and LDCs with acute/chronic problems there was a need:
  - ❐ to explore self-reliant learning and learning communities—including problem solving, peer training, shared leadership, instructional and management skills -possible use of distance learning in difficult to reach areas;
  - ❐ to encourage EFA national action plans to ensure inclusion of plans for most vulnerable populations (refugees, internally displaced person - IDPs, ISPs);
  - ❐ to revisit issues of teacher qualifications and need for low cost, large scale, high value, rapid replacement (armed conflict, HIV/AIDS, etc).
- LDCs needed strong support and technical assistance for:
  - ❐ national action plans
  - ❐ guidelines for pedagogical institutes.
- With respect to gender/diversity it was important to discuss equity alongside quality e.g. issues

related to equity of access and quality of outcomes. There was a need for:

- ❐ national action plans to address teacher and school leadership training specifically for special needs populations like linguistic and ethnic minorities and immigrants, girls and boys, disabled children;
- ❐ more comparative policy research to help inform government plans related to, for example, the impact of related national reforms and of gender equilibrium programs on role models for children.

- Regarding commitment/motivation there was a need for more comparative research related to:
  - ❐ the status of teacher codes of ethics—who drives them and why—governments, professional associations, etc. What has been the impact?
  - ❐ social respect—what changes have there been in terms of financial incentives and social rewards; any increase in social recognition and visibility through the media?
  - ❐ workload: not only need better quality indicators, but also need better understandings of what competencies are needed for teachers and school leaders to design successful teaching and learning practices.

4. ***How, Where and on What Can Partners Work Together?***

Group members indicated their readiness to consider working together by building on existing work as follows:

- Indicators: OECD; ILO; UNESCO/UIS; and IE. (NB interest varied in relation to teachers, principals and other personnel).
- Urban/rural and large/small schools: UNESCO; ASP.
- Crisis situations and LDCs: UNHCR?RET; UNESCO/EPS

- Gender/diversity; equity/quality: OREALC; IE; UNESCO; IFWU; UNHCR/RET.
- Commitment/motivation: UNESCO; IE; ILO.

5. *What are the Thematic Group's Main Conclusions?*

(i) Give some priority to the identification of good practice, the preparation of guidelines and research.

(ii) Use web site as collaborative work site and contribute guidelines, best practices, research

11

Conclusions and Outcomes of the Meeting

In the first session of day 3, the Rapporteurs presented extended versions of their reports to the plenary group. In the course of discussion, several points and issues emerged in relation to secondary education, including the following:

- the need to improve data collection and dissemination;
- the need to enhance policy dialogue between agencies;
- the need to share the conclusions of this meeting with other Inter-agency consultative groups;
- the importance of involving teachers in educational research;
- the need to consult with youth representatives via conferences.

The final session discussed outcomes and ways forward. It was recognised that the specific ideas mentioned by the Thematic Groups would be considered for further action by those involved. More generally, the following principal outcomes, were agreed in the form of recommendations to the Group itself:

1. Develop Alternative Delivery Systems

The importance of alternative delivery systems was

emphasised by many participants, so much so that, in effect, it became a fifth theme of the meeting. As indicated in the Thematic Groups, several members were committed to work in this field. Specific issues and ideas included:

- investigate the costs of various alternative delivery methods, including distance education, compared with each other and with conventional approaches;
- one important initiative here is the evaluation of distance learning in secondary education in Latin America;
- exploring further the possibilities for collaboration to identify and share successful practice;
- highlight this aspect on the GINIE web site;
- explore possible links with the 2003 information summit meeting.

2. *Enhance the Exchange of Information*

There was broad consensus that the Group's basic original objective *'to exchange information and ideas'* continued to be its fundamental rationale and was being achieved on an ongoing basis. The Conference and GINIE web sites were very successful and offered considerable opportunities for enhancing information exchange. For instance, when this meeting's details were posted, they would contain participants' e-mail addresses and their organisation's web sites thus promoting individual and group exchange.

3. *Add the Voices of Youth*

Specific suggestions for extending information exchange were:

- to include the voices of others, especially youth and practitioners/teachers;
- to develop and extend existing think tanks and conferences to embrace these ideas;

- to explore electronic forums as means of including other voices, for example on curriculum reform at secondary level.

4. *Work Towards Clarification of Key Concepts in Secondary Education*

The meeting had confirmed the central importance of adolescence in secondary education. It was agreed that key concepts could be most profitably clarified and applied in relation to practical projects, for example on:

- life-skills and adolescence;
- individual counselling.

5. *Develop Indicators of Secondary Education*

The importance of sound and reliable data was re-affirmed and several gaps were identified in the Thematic Groups. It was, accordingly, agreed that more work should be done to develop indicators on secondary education, for example, from a youth perspective.

6. *Develop Guidelines on New Roles and Training*

There was agreement that the development of practical guidelines aimed various practitioners, including teacher trainers, was an effective means of identifying and sharing successful practice. Specifically, it was suggested that they be developed for three groups:

- teachers;
- school leaders;
- other school personnel.

7. *Explore and Develop Twinning*

There was widespread support for exploring the idea of twinning, especially with countries in crisis or emergency situations, as a means of promoting the exchange of practical experience and good practice. Three initial target groups were identified:

- students;
- teachers;
- schools.

8. Collaborate on the Preparation of 47th Conference on International Education (CIE/ICE)

As indicated above, the IBE proposed that this Interagency Consultative Group work jointly for the preparation of the 47th session of the International Conference on Education (ICE) which will focus on many aspects of secondary education.

12

Future of the Consultative Group

The last session concluded with consideration of the future of this Consultative Group. By general agreement, it was fulfilling useful functions for its members. There was some discussion about its name and of the feasibility and desirability of extending its membership. It was agreed that:

- the arrangement of convening meetings of the Group on an occasional basis should be adopted;
- updating progress reports would be contributed every two years on the GINIE web site through UNESCO Headquarters;
- that Group members (or representatives of the whole group) would contribute to specific events on Secondary and Youth Affairs (e.g. the December 2002 Oman Conference and the 47th International Conference on Education).

Finally, in closing the meeting, the Chairman, Mr Iwamoto, thanked all the participants, together with the UNESCO support staff, for contributing to such a successful event.

ANNEXES

1. Agenda

Rationale:

Original Objectives of the Group

- to exchange information and ideas

3. Diversifying delivery: distance education and alternative delivery systems

[Presenters: Mr T. Linden, World Bank

Ms S. Phillips, COL

Mr B. Loing, ICDE

4. Plenary Discussion

4 pm Coffee break

Chair: Ms Sonia Bahri, UNESCO

4.30 pm Introduction to Themes
Overview:

(2 presentations of 5 minutes each per theme)
Theme 1: Meeting the Needs of Adolescents
[Presenters: Mr A. Guerrero, UNICEF
Mr Zhou Nanzhao, UNESCO, Bangkok]
Theme 2: Reforming the Curriculum: Content, Examination and Accreditation
[Presenters: Ms C. Braslavsky, IBE
Ms H. Drennen, IBO]
Theme 3: Linking Secondary Education and Technical and Vocational Education (TVE)
[Presenters: Mr P. McKenzie, OECD
Mr R. McClusky, USAID]
Theme 4: The Changing Roles of Teachers, Principals and other School Personnel
[Presenters: Ms M. Fouilhoux, EI

Mr R. Bolam, University of Cardiff]

Briefing for the four Thematic Groups

6 pm Cocktail

Wednesday, 27 March 2002

9.30 am		Thematic Group sessions[1]
	-Group 1:	Meeting the Needs of Adolescents Facilitator: Ms M.H. Henriques-Mueller, UNESCO Rapporteur: Ms S. Gear, The British Council
	-Group 2:	Reforming the Curriculum: Content, Examinations and Accreditation Facilitator: Mr J. Wimberley, Council of Europe Rapporteur: Ms F. Sauvage, IFUW
	-Group 3:	Linking Secondary Education and TVE Facilitator: Mr T. Linden, World Bank Rapporteur: Mr R. Maclean, UNESCO
	-Group 4:	The Roles of Teachers, Principals and other School Personnel Facilitator: Mr W. Ratteree, ILO Rapporteur: Ms M. McClure, University of Pittsburgh
11 am		Coffee break
11.30 am		Thematic Group sessions (cont'd)
1 pm		Lunch break
2.30		Thematic Group sessions (cont'd)
4 pm		Coffee break

Chair: Mr Wataru Iwamoto, UNESCO

4.30	Plenary Discussion Coordination of the conclusions of the four thematic groups
6 pm	End of afternoon session Meeting of Rapporteurs

Thursday, 28 March 2002

Chair: Ms Sonia Bahri, UNESCO

9.30 am	Plenary session:

United States of America/Etats-Unis d'Amérique (USAID), Mr Robert S. McClusky, Programme Manager, US Agency for International Development (USAID), G/HCD-USAID; Room 3.09-081, 1300 Pennsylvania Ave., N.W., Washington, D.C. 20523-3901, United States of America, E-mail: rmcclusky@usaid.gov

Mr Benjamin Alvarez, Education Specialist, US Agency for International Development (USAID), 1300 Pennsylvania Ave., N.W., Washington, D.C. 20523-3901, United States of America, E-mail: balvarez@usaid.gov

3. Non-Governmental Organisations/Organisations non gouvernementales

Education International (EI)/Internationale de l'Education (IE), Ms Monique Fouilhoux, Education Co-ordinator, Education International, 5, Boulevard du Roi Albert II, 1210 Brussels, Belgium, E-mail: monique.fouilhoux@ei.ie.org

International Baccalaureate Organisation (IBO)/ Organisation du baccalauréat international (OBI), Ms Helen Drennen, Director of Academic Affairs Curriculum and Assessment Centre, International Baccalaureate Organisation (IBO), Malthouse Avenue, Cardiff Gate, Cardiff CF23 8GL, United Kingdom, E-mail: helend@ibo.org

International Council for Open and Distance Education (ICDE)/Conseil international pour l'éducation ouverte et à distance (CIED), M. Bernard Loing, Représentant général auprés de l'UNESCO, Conseil international pour l'éducation ouverte et à distance, (CIED), 5, rue Jean-Carries, 75007 Paris, France, E-mail: b.loing@noos.fr

International Federation of University Women (IFUW)/ Fédération internationale des femmes diplômées des universités (FIFDU), Ms Françoise Sauvage, Representative to UNESCO, International Federation of University Women (IFUW), 29, quai de Bourbon, 75004 Paris, France, E-mail: fr.sauvage@wanadoo.fr

Refugee Education Trust (RET), Ms Marina Anselme, Associate Education Officer, Refugee Education Trust, UNHCR Headquarters, Case postale 2500, 1211 Geneva 2, Depot, Switzerland, E-mail: LOPEZ@unhcr.ch; marinalc@hotmail.com

4. Other Participants/Autres Participants

Commission nationale française pour l'UNESCO, M. Jean-Pierre Boyer, Secrétaire général, Commission nationale française pour l'UNESCO, 57, boulevard des Invalides, 75700 Paris 07 SP, France, E-mail: jean-pierre.boyer@diplomatie.fr

M. Jean Pierre Régnier, Secrétaire général adjoint, Commission nationale française pour l'UNESCO, 57, boulevard des Invalides, 75700 Paris 07 SP, France, E-mail: jean-pierre.reginer@diplomatie.fr

The British Council, Ms Sally Gear, Regional Education and Training Advisor, The British Council, 10 Spring Gardens, London SW1A 2BN, United Kingdom, E-mail: sally.gear@britishcouncil.org

University of Cardiff/Université de Cardiff, Mr Raymond Bolam (Rapporteur), Professor of Education, School of Social Sciences, Cardiff University, 65 Effingham Road, St Andrews, Bristol BF65 AY, United Kingdom, E-mail: raybolam@blueyonder.ac.uk

University of Pittsburgh/Université de Pittsburgh, Ms Maureen W. McClure, Director, GINIE Project, International Institute for Studies in Education, School of Education, 5K01 Forbes Quadrangle, University of Pittsburgh, 350 Thackery Hall, Pittsburgh, PA 15260, United States of America, E-mail: mmcclure@pitt.edu; mwmlbr@verizon.net

5. Observers/Observateurs

International Federation of University Women (IFUW)/ Fédération internationale des femmes diplômées des universités (FIFDU), Mme Michelle Broutier, Observateur, Fédération internationale des femmes

Ms Leslie Limage [listed under Rapporteurs], Section for Support for Countries in Crisis and Reconstruction (ED/EPS/CCR), E-mail: l.limage@unesco.org

Mr Mohamed Radi, Chief, Section for Support for National Educational Development (ED/EPS/NED), E-mail: m.radi@unesco.org

Division of Higher Education (ED/HED)/Division de l'enseignement supérieur, Mr K. Francisco Seddoh, Director, E-mail: f.seddoh@unesco.org

Ms Mariana Patru, Section for Teacher Education Development (ED/HED/TED), E-mail: m.patru@unesco.org

Division for the Promotion of Quality Education (ED/PEQ)/Division de la promotion de la qualité de l'éducation, Ms Mary Joy Pigozzi, Director, E-mail: mjpigozzi@unesco.org

Mr Vinayagum Chinapah, ED/PEQ/OD, E-mail: v.chinapah@unesco.org

Division of Secondary, Technical and Vocational Education (ED/STV)/Division de l'enseignement secondaire, technique et professionnel, Mr Wataru Iwamoto [listed under Secretariat], Director, E-mail: w.iwamoto@unesco.org

Ms Sonia Bahri [listed under Secretariat], Chief, Section for General Secondary Education, (ED/STV/GSE), E-mail: s.bahri@unesco.org

Ms Jamsheeda Khan-Mellor [listed under Rapporteurs], ED/STV/GSE, E-mail: j.khan-mellor@unesco.org

Mr Mohan Perera, Chief, Section for Technical and Vocational Education, (ED/STV/TVE), E-mail: m.perera@unesco.org

Mr Orlando Hall-Rose, Chief, Section for Science and Technology Education, (ED/STV/STE), E-mail: o.hall-rose@unesco.org

Other Sectors/Autres Secteurs

Bureau of Strategic Planning/Bureau de la stratégie de la planification (BSP), Ms Maria Helena Henriques-

Mueller, Chief, Youth Coordination Unit (BSP/WYS/UCJ), Division of Women, Youth and Special Strategies, (BSP/WYS), E-mail: mh.henriques-mueller@unesco.org

Mr Jean-Yves Le Saux, Division of Programme Planning, Monitoring and Reporting, (BSP/PMR), E-mail: jy.le-saux@unesco.org

UNESCO Consultant, Ms Vittoria Cavicchioni, 23, rue Auguste Vitu, 75015 Paris, France, E-mail: cavicchioni@noos.fr

Other Observers/Autres Observateurs

Mr Marie Bardin, Assistant Programme Specialist, ED/PEQ/ASP, m.bardin@unesco.org

Ms Sabine Detzel, Programme Specialist, BSP/UC, d.detzel@unesco.org

Ms Koto Kanno, Programme Specialist, ED/BAS, k.kanno@unesco.org

Ms Elizabeth Khawajkie, Coordinator, ED/PEQ/ASP, e.khawjkie@unesco.org

Ms Linda King, Senior Programme Specialist, ED/PEQ/VAL, l.king@unesco.org

Mr Chang-shin Kwack, Programme Specialist, ED/STV/TVE, Cs.Kwack@unesco.org

Ms Miki Nozawa, Assistant Programme Specialist, ED/STV/TVE, m.nozawa@unesco.org

Ms Antonella Verdiani, Programme Specialist, ED/PEQ/VAL, a.verdiani@unesco.org

NOTES

1. During the morning session each group should consider the theme's implications for the post-Dakar agenda. During the afternoon session each Group should

- identify areas where more research/action is needed
- suggest joint projects/publications for the next two years
- reach agreement on Group Rapporteur's draft report.

13

General Secondary Education in the Twenty-First Century: Trends, Challenges and Priorities

Prof. J. Michel Leclercq

I. Key Problems

It is proposed that three key problems, which are not only fundamental but interdependent, be subjected to analysis: the impact of the new social and economic context, the ways in which attendance has been increased and the consequence of that increase, and the forms of modernisation to be considered. There is justification on at least two counts for taking these as the key problems. First, all three correspond to deep-seated developments, which, if not already underway, are at least foreseeable – developments connected with essential issues of general secondary-school education, either in its aims or its modes of operation, elements which are almost always at issue when concern to adopt new directions and scenarios arises. Second, at the methodological level, the analysis of each of these problems simultaneously entails the assessment of current situations, the making of future projections or comparisons between the situations in the various education systems, and the foregrounding, in each case, of a particular perspective, given the nature of the object and its specific characteristics. In examining the impact of context, we may clearly expect to see assessments and comparisons accorded a leading role, whereas in examining efforts at modernisation we shall rightly expect to see a forward-looking perspective, doubtless as a result of the disappointing assessments to which many attempts at innovation give rise.

1. *The Impact of the New Economic and Social Context*

We might consider the need to accord particular attention to the impact of developments in the economic and social context- developments which are, as we know, always crucial to any kind of education or training.

It is, however, beyond doubt that these developments have come to have an even more decisive impact on general secondary-school education, on account of the role this is expected to play both in training the personnel required for the economy and in training the citizens who have to form today's societies. The question of raising the skills level for entry into the labour market is not simply an issue for technical or vocational secondary education, but also for general education - not least because solid, broadly-based knowledge and also generic skills, such as the ability to communicate, now form the basis of all requisite work skills. It also falls to general secondary education to develop in young people those attitudes which contribute to the proper functioning of societies, such as civic sense or tolerance. These points were highlighted by the International Commission on Education for the Twentieth-first Century, which stated: "It is now generally recognised that, for economic growth to take place, a high proportion of the population has to have received secondary education".[1] It was also argued, at the Dakar World Education Forum, that: "No country can be expected to develop into a modern and open economy without having a certain proportion of its work force completing secondary education".[2] The same Forum's report on Europe and North America pointed out that: "with the development of knowledge and of its influence on the lives of people, basic education takes more time: in our countries, it covers at least lower secondary education."[3] It is, however, probable that this standpoint will soon cease to be the preserve of the most prosperous countries and that more and more regions will come to share it, given the deep and rapid changes the economic and social context is set to undergo.

As a result, there is need both of a forward-looking approach to the economic and social context and of a vision for general secondary education in the future. In particular, we have to appreciate the need for secondary education to be expanded at a rate faster than some have previously felt necessary. For example, a development of production techniques in which intellectual operations take precedence over manual operations on account of the massive introduction of new technologies may lead to questioning the wisdom of retaining vocational training within the lower secondary school, when this may deprive pupils of the requisite range of general knowledge. In time, vocational training in the upper secondary school may ultimately come to be questioned in a similar way, as happened in Japan in the 1980s.

It goes without saying, however, that the analysis of context cannot merely consist in identifying overwhelming trends to which we must necessarily submit. Among those trends, we have to differentiate between what is acceptable and what is not. Only if general secondary education stands impotently by, or colludes with the development, will unscrupulous productivism or unbridled consumerism result. And it must indeed show its determination to help young people to resist all the forms of excess or deviance in the surrounding environment.

We should not forget, too, that secondary education provides its own context. It is always possible, through system effects or by the action of pressure groups, for the administrative and pedagogical organisation of that education to set itself up as the equivalent of an external, independent reality, promoting certain conceptions or practices and thwarting others. This explains, for example, why thoroughly sound projects may fail for want of sufficient understanding of the attitudes and behaviour of education officers, teachers, families or pupils. It may be that this phenomenon applies more to general secondary education than to other sectors, on account of the importance society attributes to that sector or the importance it attributes to itself under the influence of a persistent elitism.

The relations between general secondary-school education and its context, are then, highly complex. There must be a concern to investigate and decipher these relations, both in order to be able to explain situations as products of natural, legitimate influences, and also to detect excesses or anomalies which may generate what are in some cases tragic misconceptions and illusions.

2. *Mass Secondary Enrolment, Democratisation and Equity*

In the operation of general secondary education over the last two or three decades the most striking phenomenon has been the very great increase in enrolment levels.

As can be seen from the statistics in the table below, in the Member States represented at this meeting the increase between 1970 and 1997 has been spectacular. In many countries, total enrolments have risen by a factor of two or three, and in some cases far more. It is evident that this process is universal among the countries concerned, since it occurs in both the richest and the most deprived of them. And it shows up even more clearly when we remember that, in the countries of Europe as a whole, enrolment figures in upper secondary education have virtually doubled since 1980.

This development has comparable causes in the sample of systems selected for examination at this meeting and on a much wider scale. One essential factor in the shift to mass secondary education has been the inclusion of lower secondary-school education in compulsory schooling. In almost all cases those countries concerned to make up for previous backwardness in this area, such as Bangladesh and China, have extended the length of compulsory education to nine years. However, a similar extension of compulsory schooling has also occurred in recent years in many industrialised countries, showing the same concern on the part of governments to provide young people with the basic education required by the changes in the economy and society. For identical reasons, in those years of upper secondary education which are not part of compulsory schooling, families—often encouraged by governments—choose to have their children carry on their studies. Though this trend is much more marked in the northern hemisphere, it also exists in the South.

In these conditions, it is quite clear that the profile and purposes of general secondary-school education change profoundly. It is no longer reserved, as in the past, for the minority of the most fortunate youth. Nor is it any longer the prime aim of secondary education to afford access to higher studies, even if that remains very much a goal. It must provide the skills with which to enter working life, and must in many cases do so for the majority of pupils. Many still begin their working lives at the end of lower secondary education, but increasingly often they now do so at the end of upper secondary schooling. With the advent of mass secondary enrolment, we have seen a different form of secondary education established, with a new clientele and new missions to fulfil.

However, it is equally obvious that this—theoretically compulsory—enrolment in lower secondary, or voluntary enrolment in upper secondary, education is far from representing a merely utilitarian decision on the part of governments or users, dictated by the demands of the economy (and by a concern to escape unemployment, in particular). They are also looking for a more democratic, more equitable operation of the education system, in which access to secondary education no longer restricted to an elite or to the most privileged social groups. This is particularly the case with lower secondary education, which has become an integral part of a common core of education—something long called for in many countries across the whole political spectrum and within all social groups. But the attitude towards upper secondary education is not radically different. Access to "high school" is regarded as a symbol of social advancement virtually the world over. This explains the disaffection which may be felt with vocational training at the upper secondary level - that form of training not being seen as part of "proper high-school education". How else are we to explain the low enrolment figures in vocational education in the table below or the fact that enrolment figures for such training did not rise in Europe until the continent experienced a long period of very high unemployment among the 18-24 age-group?

Enrolment in Secondary Education 1970-1997

Country	*1970*	*1980*	*1990-1991*	*1993-1997*
Bangladesh		T. 2,142,335 F 606,913	T. 3,156,119 F. 1,070,000	
Canada	T. 1,636,913 F. 799,141		T. 2,292,497 F. 1,118,112	T. 2,505,389 F. 1,218,403
China	T. 26,482,976		T. 52,385,600 F. 21,706,500 V. 2,150,400	T. 71,883,000 F. 32,530,000
Guinea	T. 59,918 F. 13,064 V. 2,013		T. 85,942 F. 20,929 V. 8,202	T. 153,661 F. 39,449
Lebanon	T. 159,871 F. 64,141 V. 2,590		T. 248,097 F. 131,352 V. 37,403	T. 347,850 F. 179,629
Mexico	T. 1,584,342 F. 609,969 V. 423,584		T. 6,704,297 F. 3,163,293	T. 7,631,605 F. 3,407,756
Russia	T. 11,351,000 F. 5,735,000 V. 1,399,000		T. 12,363,000 F. 6,300,000 V. 1,252,000	T. 12,424,000 F. 6,399,000 V. 1,007,000
South Africa	T. 542,194 F. 264,461		T. 2,742,105 F. 1,474,611	T. 3,749,449 F. 2,039,551

Key: T – total enrolment
F – female enrolment
V – enrolment in vocational secondary education
Source: *UNESCO Statistical Yearbook* (except in the case of Bangladesh, where the sources used are national statistics).

We must, however, remind the reader that the actual situations produced by the expansion of general secondary-school education may be very far removed from the advances in democratisation and equity expected.

Certain groups are still frequently sidelined. As is well known, outside Europe, North America and Japan, access to general secondary-school education and, even more to technical education remains difficult for girls. And everywhere, irrespective of sex, children from economically deprived or socially stigmatised groups and those suffering physical or mental handicaps suffer overt or concealed forms of segregation. Conversely, the systematic provision of general secondary-school education to all youngesters may leave some facing patterns of study which expose them to failure, or bring them very limited opportunities for socio-professional inclusion. When this is the case, instead of providing a fairer distribution of opportunity, the expansion of general secondary-school education may produce new social divisions.

Furthermore, mass secondary enrolment has not always been accompanied by allocation of the necessary resources to provide adequate conditions for learning. There may not be a sufficiently close-knit network of educational establishments to prevent children from having to make long, inconvenient journeys to school. Some subjects may be neglected or ignored for want of sufficient staff, or staff with the necessary skills, to teach them. A shortage of buildings or teachers may mean classes are overcrowded. These are defects which would be harmful in any conditions, but they are particularly harmful for those we might term the "new pupils" of the secondary sector, who need the best possible school environment to adapt to a new world and achieve good results in it. Here, again, these problems mainly affect lower secondary education, and we know that the considerable difficulties sometimes experienced there relate largely to a lack of material and human resources being brought on stream to deal with the many problems generated by the introduction of compulsory enrolment. Upper secondary education is, however, already facing the same problems, and will do so increasingly as rolls increase.

3. The Need for Modernisation and Innovation

A third aspect of general secondary education with which we must concern ourselves is the modernisation of that education through major innovations in its modes of operation and teaching methods. These are processes from which it cannot really remain aloof, given the many adaptations currently being required of it – adaptations it would hardly be possible to make without breaking with approaches which have often remained unchanged for many years. Modernisation has to be brought about if the many adaptations required are to be achieved: adaptation to the development of knowledge and to technological advance; adaptation to secondary education's new clientele; adaptation to the new roles that education has to play in societies. Modernisation and innovation must be achieved in practically every sector.

First and foremost, the syllabus needs to be modernised. The place of certain disciplines in the syllabus must be upgraded—disciplines which have always been taught, but which today require particular attention, either to update their content, as in the sciences and technology, or to raise their profile, as in the case of language-teaching. Room has also to be made for subjects which have until now been virtually ignored, such as the new information and communication technologies, civics, and inter-cultural or sexual education, not to mention increased provision for artistic culture or physical and sporting activities. But we have even to rethink the notion of syllabus or curriculum so that young people may benefit from teaching and education in which all the elements are inter-linked and related to all the components of their person and their existence. This is all the more necessary when preparation for working life has become as important in secondary education as preparation for higher studies. And this problem by no means relates merely to the countries of the

South where a secondary qualification is supposed to open other doors than those of the university. In the North, at least 20% of pupils do not obtain a leaving qualification and have to face career paths which may often be complex and arduous. Secondary education must equip them too with other assets than a passport to university.

We are also increasingly aware that changes in content must be accompanied by changes in teaching methods. The methods which prevailed in the past were based largely on teacher authoritarianism and pupil passivity. The disadvantages of these methods are now clear for all to see. First, they are detrimental to a section of the school population which is poorly prepared to fit into a mould which favours theoretical and intellectualist styles entirely alien to the approaches prevalent in the social groups from which a large fraction of secondary pupils now come. But, most importantly, these methods are ill-adapted to the conditions for knowledge and skills-acquisition as revealed by the cognitive sciences; they are also inappropriate in view of the possibilities opened up by the new vehicles of information and communication. There can be no passive reception. It is by active discovery and exchange that we learn. We can no longer be content with teaching through unidirectional messages, teaching focussed solely on the pupil's brain. We have now to concern ourselves with the whole person and his/her diversity.

We could not hope to do this either if secondary schools did not also radically modify their modes of operation. This involves, first, the adoption of new ways of working by teachers to impart the requisite dynamism and flexibility to learning - failing which, teachers and pupils alike run the risk of delusion, boredom and failure. Second, it involves the formation of educational teams which are open to the entire educational community, and hence not merely made up of teachers. This is one of the essential conditions for responding to pupil needs in all areas, giving them all the time they need and showing an ability to listen. It also involves a new governance of schools, in which democratically based rules of conduct and, above all, rules of life should prevail – rules adopted as far as possible through dialogue and participation. It is difficult to see how we can otherwise offer the requisite secondary education to people who are not the pupils of yesteryear, but young men and women determined to assert their independence and maturity.

It doubtless remains for us to ask whether lower and upper secondary education do not call for different approaches. Are there not still, particularly in lower secondary education, adolescents who ought to be shown a better lead (though this does not mean abandoning recourse, where necessary, to stricter forms of discipline)? A similar question arises with regard to what is taught. In so far as, in most education systems, lower secondary education now forms part of basic education, it seems natural that it should involve the assimilation of a single syllabus by all pupils. By contrast, as the Report of the International Commission on Education for the Twentieth-first Century stresses, upper secondary-school education must be highly diversified. It should "be the time when the most varied talents are revealed and flourish."[4] Yet it is increasingly questionable whether lower secondary education can continue to hold to an authoritarian model for its operation and a unitary model for its curriculum—features which are always likely to pose problems for some pupils. The recent measures in France to introduce more flexibility into its "common school" model are symptomatic in this regard.

Most aspects of modernisation and innovation give rise to comparable degrees of hesitancy. Indeed, this is a field in which there are many more questions than answers. Modernisation programmes have in many cases had to be redrafted in mid-stream, as all the Member States represented at this meeting will be aware. The outcomes of these programmes are often disappointing on account of the lengthy time-spans or unwieldy compromises involved. Teacher training has also seen many reform projects, but it is difficult to avoid an impression that little actual progress is being made. When an initiative leads to the conclusion that teacher training must "include, among other things... an input from other disciplines (than the one taught)... sensitisation to linguistic and cultural diversity... learning teamwork... discovering interactivity... and acquiring an awareness that pupils today are no longer willing to receive an education in the traditional sense,"[5] and when one finds a whole string of similar viewpoints expressed,[6] one is both convinced of the strength of identical concerns and yet uneasy about the actual effects achieved.

We are not, then, seeing at all clearly the emergence of those "learning organisations" which secondary schools ought, in the view of the OECD, to become if they are to meet the challenges of the new millennium, particularly as regards entry into lifelong learning. However, even more modest ambitions seem far from being satisfied. Educational teams exist more on paper than in reality. And few of their members are non-teaching staff or come from outside the school. More generally, secondary schools are not places where human resources are satisfactorily managed, even though the educational world might be thought a much more favourable setting than business for providing careers in which everyone, through the full and free deployment of their skills, would be recognised at their true worth and feel fulfilled by their work.

A further illustration of reticence and overcautiousness can be seen in the fate reserved for the self-government of schools. The idea that this is a timely development—and one which needs to be reinforced—is practically unchallenged. But self-government generally remains limited because it seldom extends to financial autonomy and, so far as the syllabus is concerned, when it comes to deciding timetables and the subjects to be taught, restrictive regulations usually apply. Conversely, self-government has only to increase for concern to surface immediately about the prospects of preserving sufficient coherence in the education system or avoiding disparities which generate inequalities in educational provision in the secondary sector.

Clearly, a vision for a secondary education modernised by thoroughgoing innovation still remains to be forged – innovation not merely confined to incorporating new resources, such as information technology, but actively employing those resources to change the practices and behaviour of teachers and pupils.

II. Reforms and Reform Strategies

The foregoing thoughts lead on naturally to the view that a serious redesign of secondary education is necessary and that such projects are in danger of running into significant obstacles, such as the complexity of the problems to be tackled or the resistance posed by existing situations.

The difficult nature of educational reforms has, in fact, become a recurring theme among educational decision-makers and practitioners. One recent writer revealingly entitled a book on the subject: *Education: An Impossible Reform?*[7] Another, in a study on the question of educational reform in sub-Saharan Africa between 1960 and 2000, stressed the ineffectiveness of efforts at change made over almost half a century.[8]

It is probable too, however, that the weariness felt at failed reform projects has provided a stimulus to reflection on the conditions in which reforms may best succeed and, more precisely, on the processes and strategies to be adopted to that end.[9]

This reflection has highlighted the following points:

A reform always requires a detailed preparatory research phase, which may extend over several years. This may seem a major obstacle in situations where reform is urgently needed, but it would be better to resort, where necessary, to a number of temporary individual measures, amounting virtually to mere treatment of the symptoms, than hastily to launch a poorly prepared project of general reform which is likely to have very harmful consequences of a deep and lasting nature.

This research phase must also be a phase of consultation with all the parties involved in the reform. The age of top-down reform is past. Today, there must be dialogue between the decision-makers and their partners (local communities, teachers, families and, increasingly now, the pupils - at least in the upper secondary sector). This process of arriving at a consensus through consultation may take a considerable time, not least because of the amount of information and communication required.

If time is needed for the preparation of reforms, it is also needed for their application, since gradual introduction of reforms is far preferable to immediate, across-the-board implementation, which may produce over-ambitious expectations or violent changes in practice of a kind likely to spark all manner of resistance.

This is also why, in the long process of implementing reform, one should not be afraid to review it or, indeed, to reform the reform itself if some of its elements seem to require revision because they are either ineffective or harmful. This, however, assumes a process of running evaluation of the reform, which is not always present.

The precautions which must accompany the preparation and implementation of reforms lead us also to ask what their pattern and scope should be? Should we consider reforming the whole of an education system at all levels and in all sectors? Or should we not have much more limited aims, relating to a well-defined area? Opinions on this question continue to differ, but some trends can be identified. Awareness of the complexity and difficulty of any reform suggests at least that reforms should be made in a particular sector and should be phased in gradually. This is preferable to launching a thoroughgoing reform at a stroke. Attention should also be given to the inevitable inter-dependency of elements. There is little sense changing teaching structures or syllabuses without a parallel reform of teacher training. But it is also becoming clearer that reforms relating to contents and methods seem to have much greater impact than reforms of the administrative or teaching structures. This explains why we are much more likely to find reforms of the syllabus or of teacher training in the secondary sector today than structural reorganisations of lower or upper secondary education. All in all, it seems to be accepted that the way of preparing and carrying out reform is as important as its content, and that a reform is, first and foremost, a strategy for change.

At all events, to be effective a reform has to meet two imperatives. It must set clearly defined, clearly prioritised objectives, which are not a shopping-list of measures but a systematic set of priorities, as few in number as possible. It must lay down the strategies to be implemented to achieve these objectives, with all that this involves in terms of the scheduling of successive interventions and permanent assessment to evaluate the results attained and those which remain to be achieved. There can be no doubt either that these demands are even more pressing in secondary education, where situations and issues have to be addressed in all their complexity, given the large numbers of people now involved and the interconnectedness of the many problems faced.

REFERENCES

1. *Learning: The Treasure Within* (Paris: UNESCO, 1996).
2. *The Dakar Framework for Action* (Paris: UNESCO, 2000), paragraph 34.
3. "Regional Framework for Action. Europe and North America", February 2000.
4. *Learning: The Treasure Within* (Paris: UNESCO, 1996).
5. *La formation des enseignants* (Paris: La Documentation Française, 2000).
6. As in the Canadian report, *Enhancing the Role of Teachers in a Changing World* (Council of Ministers of Education, Canada, 1996), p. 37.

7. Pierre Laderrière, *L'enseignement, une rèforme impossible? Analyse comparée* (Paris: L'Harmattan, 1999).
8. Amara Fofana, *La problématique de la réforme de l'éducation en Afrique subsaharienne 1960-2000*, unpublished study, BREDA/ Dakar.
9. In this connection, see *Strategies for educational reform: from concept to realisation* (Strasbourg, Council of Europe, 2000).

14

Meeting Agreements of the UNESCO International Expert Meeting on General Secondary Education in the 21st Century

International Expert Meeting on General Secondary Education in the Twenty-first Century: Trends, Challenges and Priorities, Beijing, Peoples Republic of China, 21-25 May 2001. © UNESCO. Courtesy: UNESCO.

The UNESCO international expert meeting on General Secondary Education in the twenty-first century held in Beijing, the People's Republic of China, in May 2001 reached consensus that:

- Secondary Education should be given high priority.
- The objectives and functions of secondary education need to be redefined for the twenty-first century.

The meeting then focussed on the major dilemmas Secondary Education is, or will be facing in meeting these redefined objectives and functions. These dilemmas involve the balance between mass and selective schooling, general and specialised (vocational) education and cognitive and behavioural outcomes.

In respect of mass and selective schooling, consensus was reached that:

- Countries should continue to be committed to the goal of mass Secondary Education as a minimum in terms of policy and provision.
- Commitment to universal access to Secondary Education as an aspiration should be maintained with efforts to remove barriers and obstacles as well as build on strengths and opportunities especially for girls.
- Serious attention be given to making adequate provision for those not selected into Secondary Education, those who drop out or leave before completing the cycle and those denied access to their preferred streams.
- Where there is not full transition from Primary to Secondary and/or from lower Secondary to upper Secondary, efforts must be made to accommodate all those who are eligible through alternative provisions. Where this is not possible available places should be allocated equitably and transparently.
- Mass access to Secondary Education will require partnership between governments and other providers (private, NGOs, etc.), but governments should seek to safeguard the interests of learners by ensuring quality standards are maintained by all providers.
- The structure of programmes and streaming practices should be reviewed to offer greater flexibility and choice to learners in the selection process, including the option to return to a preferred stream.
- Future orientation at Secondary should be towards greater quality and diversity of what is provided, more flexibility in the organisation of learning and greater responsiveness to the needs and circumstances of learners.

In respect of general and selective (vocational) education consensus was reached that:

- The Secondary Education system should focus on links between academic and vocational subjects and their interdependence in the overall education of adolescent learners of both genders.
- Secondary Education is about preparation for life and should reflect the reality of life in the twenty-first century that encompasses a seamless to-and-fro between continued learning and the world of work.
- The nature of vocational subjects, the way in which they are organised and taught, as well as the recognition given to them determine their status in the Secondary school curriculum.
- Secondary Education including Vocational Education needs to address not only the human resource needs of the society but also the development needs and aspirations of the individual.
- There is a strong trend in Secondary Education in most countries to include some element of Vocational Education for all learners. Some countries are experimenting with ways of providing such joint education to different population groups, including migrants, isolated rural populations and learners in regular secondary schools.
- Incorporating Vocational Education into Secondary Education can be expensive resulting in poor quality teaching and a lowering of status of these subjects. Innovative and cost-effective strategies to overcome this problem have included contracting out the teaching of subjects to nearby specialist schools and centres or creating different ways of teaching. Vocational disciplines that are less

demanding in terms of equipment, materials and practically trained instructors.

- As the trend of life-long learning is becoming clear, Secondary Education is adjusting to this reality by developing flexible structures and varied options in their programmes, as well as having stronger links to the world of work.

In respect of cognitive and behavioural outcomes, consensus was reached that:

- There is recognition that traditional academically based education does not adequately address students' needs in terms of realising their full potential, especially in a context of rapid economic, cultural and social change and gender based discrimination.
- Given the declining role of other socializing agencies schools should take greater responsibility for helping learners acquire life-skills.
- The emerging role of teachers (notably as facilitators), their status, integrity and commitment are essential for implementing life-skills education successfully. The quality of pre-service and in-service teacher training is critical in this regard.
- Teaching methods, school facilities and services should be developed and adapted to provide life-skills/behavioural education.
- The role of Secondary school principals needs to the consistent with this new reality.
- Education decision-makers need to be sensitised to the consequences of their choices based on evidence of such factors as the links between academic success and personal and community well being.
- A multi-sectoral approach involving government ministries, NGOs local communities, etc. is

essential for successful implementation of this kind of education.

Other themes identified by the meeting that Secondary Education is, or will be, facing in achieving its new objectives and functions included:

- Inclusive and compensatory education.
- Eliminate gender disparities.
- Strengthening equity.
- The effective use of information communications technology.

The meeting further agreed that the resources and/or strategies needed to respond to the new objectives and functions of Secondary Education and to manage the themes or dilemmas include:

- Commencing with the view that students are at the centre of any education reform;
- Understanding that there are three interrelated components to support students' learning – the people, whether education professionals, parents or community members, the educational policies that offer a framework for what students need to learn, and the infrastructure.

Member nations sought UNESCO's assistance in attaining the following in relation to these three interrelated components:

- For students

  (i) Reconstructing Secondary Education to ensure a consideration of learners' diversified needs and provide them with knowledge and life-long skills including vocational learning;

- For teachers, curriculum and school:

  (i) Giving priority to teacher education (pre-service and in-service);

(ii) Ensuring that the curricula present goals and objectives clearly and precisely and reflect local needs – including socio-economic needs;

(iii) Ensuring schools both understand and have the ability to become learning organisations/learning communities.

- For infrastructure and policy:

(i) Ensuring that policy-makers stress and give enough attention to Secondary Education;

(ii) Providing access to Secondary Education by providing a place for all learners;

(iii) Offering appropriate resources for Secondary Education through adequate budget allocations.

Specific suggestions for future UNESCO activities centred on:

- Providing written case studies and/or a data base of best/successful practice in Secondary Education with a focus on issues identified at this meeting

(i) Vocational Education,

(ii) distance learning and information communications technology,

(iii) life-skills and life-long education,

(iv) discovery learning,

(v) the changing role of teachers and the use of roles other than teachers in schools,

(vi) pre-service and in-service teacher education and increasing the status of teachers,

(vii) assessment literacy (i.e., having and being able to use assessment with predictive validity) and evidence-informed policy and accountability,

(viii) capacity building or organisational learning/ learning community,

(ix) whole-of-government approaches to policy and practice,

(x) the balance between administrative, budgeting and curriculum centralisation and decentralisation,

(xi) complementary and alternative provision of resources.

- Organise forums and facilitating international exchange and cooperation in the area of Secondary Education leading to a major World Education Forum on Secondary Education;
- Continue to provide a vehicle for establishing the ideals for Secondary Education in the twenty-first century and for holding governments accountable for moving towards these ideals.